Rosie Waterland is an author, con... ...screenwriter. Her first book, *The Anti Cool Girl* (HarperCollins, 2015), was a critically acclaimed national bestseller, shortlisted for an Indie Book Award and two ABIA Awards in 2016, and also shortlisted for the 2017 Russell Award for Humour Writing.

Rosie is currently developing her own television series and is a contributing writer for various other Australian TV shows. Rosie debuted her first live one-woman show at the Melbourne International Comedy Festival in March 2016, called *My Life On The Couch (With Vodka)*, and then took the show on a sold-out national tour in October of the same year. Her second one-woman show, *Crazy Lady*, will be touring Australia in September 2017.

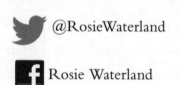

@RosieWaterland

Rosie Waterland

Praise for *The Anti-Cool Girl*:

'Hilarious, wise, gutsy, clear-eyed, devastating and uplifting.
It's a marvel.'
Richard Glover

'Waterland's writing is ... individual, wounded,
brilliant and hilarious'
Sydney Morning Herald

'If Augusten Burroughs and Lena Dunham abandoned
their child in an Australian housing estate, she'd write this
heartbreaking, hilarious book.'
Dominic Knight, *The Chaser*

every lie i've ever told

rosie waterland

FOURTH ESTATE
An Imprint of HarperCollins*Publishers*

Fourth Estate
An imprint of HarperCollins*Publishers*

First published in Australia in 2017
by HarperCollinsPublishers Australia Pty Limited
ABN 36 009 913 517
harpercollins.com.au

HarperCollins*Publishers*
Level 13, 201 Elizabeth Street, Sydney NSW 2000, Australia
Unit D1, 63 Apollo Drive, Rosedale, Auckland 0632, New Zealand
A 53, Sector 57, Noida, UP, India
1 London Bridge Street, London, SE1 9GF, United Kingdom
2 Bloor Street East, 20th floor, Toronto, Ontario M4W 1A8, Canada
195 Broadway, New York NY 10007, USA

ISBN 978 1 4607 5065 0 (pbk)
ISBN 978 1 4607 0523 0 (e-book)

Cover design by Hazel Lam, HarperCollins Design Studio
Cover image of Rosie Waterland © Patrick Boland
Typeset in Bembo Std by Kirby Jones
Printed and bound in Australia by McPhersons Printing Group
The papers used by HarperCollins in the manufacture of this book are a natural, recyclable product made from wood grown in sustainable plantation forests. The fibre source and manufacturing processes meet recognised international environmental standards, and carry certification.

WARNING

Every Lie I've Ever Told deals with themes of mental illness, self-harm and suicide. My comedy-addled brain means I don't know how to write without putting a joke on every page, but parts of this story may still be triggering to some people, which I completely understand and empathise with. Resources have been provided at the back of this book if you feel like you need to reach out.

for Antonio

Contents

I knew I'd officially hit rock bottom when somebody's shit splattered the curtain of the hospital bed next to mine. A nurse had mercifully thought to pull it across at the last second, perhaps predicting in her frontline experience that an emergency-room enema can sometimes result in a projectile faeces situation. And let me tell you: this enema did. It really, really did.

I've never seen anything quite like it. One second, I was lying in my bed, barely noticing the shadowy silhouettes busy at work through the curtain. The next, I heard a moan, then a gasp, and then ... It almost seemed fake, the way it sprayed perfectly and gratuitously across the curtain, the sound it made as it hit the fabric, the slow drips down to the floor.

It was the clichéd way blood splatters on walls in B-grade horror movies.

Except it was shit.

And it was just left there for hours, so I could either keep the curtain open and look in awe at the man it had all come out

1

of, or I could keep the curtain closed and look at the shit itself. I alternated.

How had my life ended up at this point? How had I, at thirty, in the middle of what was easily the most successful and brilliant time of my life – except for maybe when I was cast as Little Red Rocking Hood in my Year 6 production of *Little Red Rocking Hood* – how had I ended up in the emergency room next to a B-grade horror movie enema poo blast?

Surely this was someone else's life? Surely it was someone else who had downed all that vodka followed by so many pills? Surely it was someone else who was now lying in this bed, hooked up to a million drips, barely able to breathe through the physical pain in her body that didn't even compare to the emotional pain in her brain? Surely it was someone else who had just witnessed 3am projectile enema poo?

This wasn't me. It couldn't be. I was successful. I had overcome, damn it. I WAS A FREAKING PHOENIX WHO HAD RISEN FROM THE FREAKING ASHES. My first book said so! My first book ended with me finding myself, with me leaving my mental-health struggles firmly in the past with my traumatic childhood. Whatever hardship I had faced, I had beaten it. I had won. Bestselling book. National tour. TV show in the works. My fridge broke and I could afford to buy a new one (like, a brand-new one – no more driving three hours like a chump to pick up 1980s whitegoods found on Gumtree). I had *made it*. All my dreams had come true, I had an operating fridge, I was doing brilliantly, and I had written the memoir to prove it. I even had online haters.

I had conquered life at thirty, and nothing was ever going to go wrong again!

What a total fraud.

And as I lay in that hospital bed, the remains of the enema poo on one side of me and concerned friends on the other, the same few thoughts kept going through my head. First, that the nurses all wore very fancy Nikes and it was brilliant product placement because now I really wanted a pair. Second, that I really wanted to remember what episode of *Will & Grace* the Subway Tush song came from, because I was singing it in my head over and over and over and over. And third, how ironic it was that right in the middle of writing my second book, a book about all the random lies I've told in my life, I'd ended up telling the most significant lie of all.

I haven't spent hours online designing my wedding to nobody.
(I have. More than once. Oh god.)

There is a secret folder on my computer. I created it a few years ago, when I realised my embarrassing secret needed to be contained, and contained quietly. Nobody knows about the folder, because if they did I would need to move to one of those witness protection towns in middle America where men who work at service stations are always chewing on a single piece of hay and wear overalls with a red handkerchief hanging out of the back pocket. That's how far I'd have to go.

The folder is labelled 'Rosie's Tax Invoices', but I'm a thirty-year-old with a Polly Pocket collection, so obviously I don't actually keep my tax invoices organised in a folder on my desktop (why would I spend time doing things like my taxes when I could be on eBay looking for the 1993 Fairylight Wonderland edition that actually lights up?).

No – the 'tax' label is a genius and complex ruse, designed to keep prying eyes from snooping at my secret shame. You know how people panic about their internet history getting into the wrong hands? Everybody laughs and says, 'If I die nobody let my mum see my internet history! *cheeky wink*' But behind the laughter, everybody is secretly anxious about that time they typed 'microwave popcorn foot tampon sex thing' into Google.

(And hey, I get it. We've all been in that weird, depressed place, when the show you've been binge-watching is over, and the hole it leaves in your life feels like a death. Then, in an attempt to fill the vast emptiness of the post binge-watching void, you start searching all the actors who were in the show on Wikipedia, then you're shocked that one of them is the brother of the guy who wrote that other show, and that show is based on that famous conspiracy from the 1960s, and that conspiracy started when that woman was kidnapped by that psycho, and psychopathy has a test you can take now to see if you are one, and you aren't one but you reckon that girl from high school is, and after looking at her Facebook page you find yourself on her first boyfriend's new wife's page, where you see that meme with Kermit drinking tea making a joke about a weird sex fetish, and when you go to tag someone underneath you see that someone else has tagged a friend and written 'lol remember the microwave popcorn foot tampon sex thing??' so then you google 'microwave popcorn foot tampon sex thing', and not only do you see some weird stuff, but you suddenly realise you've been online for six hours.)

(Or you just sat down at your computer one day and typed in 'microwave popcorn foot tampon sex thing', because that's your jam and you're not ashamed. In which case, good for you, please continue living your best life.)

The secret folder is the one thing on my computer I panic about people seeing, and it's not even filled with freaky porn that is slowly stopping me from being able to orgasm normally.

The folder on my computer labelled 'Rosie's Tax Invoices' is actually filled with … Oh god. I hate myself. It's filled with wedding stuff.

So. Much. Wedding. Stuff. I actually kind of wish it *was* freaky porn.

I honestly don't even know how it started. I just found a picture online of a ring I liked one day, and before I knew it, I was making fake folders and disguising jpegs and signing up to the Vera Wang website. There have been times I've turned down social invitations because I was so far down a Pinterest 'funky table setting' rabbit hole that it just didn't feel worth it to leave the house.

The folder would easily have at least five hundred pictures in it by now, although I stopped counting a while ago. Engagement rings, flowers, wedding dresses, invitations, bridesmaids' gowns, shoes, suits for the groom, lighting, food … I've got it all covered in my folder of lies.

This thing goes so deep, there is actually wedding *Inception* on my laptop now – just like the folder they are hidden in, each jpeg has its own special name so as to avoid detection. That oval diamond with the dainty gold band? 'Editorial Meeting June 2013'. The Christian Siriano dress with the sleeves I like? 'Payslip May 2016'.

'Rosie's Tax Invoices' is like the Bermuda Triangle of shame on my computer – I can't go in there without my dignity disappearing.

But how did I end up here? How did I end up knee-deep in a creepy cesspool of wedding-picture shame?

I was never the little girl who cared about weddings, or anything girly, really. While other little ladies were dressed as princesses, I was kicking a kid out of my birthday party for refusing to concede that the Ninja Turtles were better than Batman (they were and continue to be and I won't hear another word about it). While my sister was in her room with friends putting on make-up and dancing to Ace of Base, I was curled up in bed reading *Goosebumps*, waiting for *Seinfeld* to come on TV so I could tape it onto a blank VHS.

I was definitely not the girl who owned a frilly scrapbook with the words 'Dream Day' written on the cover with glitter glue. But now I have the equivalent of that scrapbook on my laptop, just waiting to be filled with inspo photos from the Spring/Summer 2017 Monique Lhuillier collection.

So why the hell have I spent a sickening amount of hours, all through my twenties, planning a wedding that is not actually real? I like being single! (Honestly. I'm not saying that while my eye twitches in panic.) When you're single, you can take your laptop to the toilet without judgement. It's heaven.

So while I'm not desperate for a wedding, the *Inception*-level cave of frilly shame in 'Rosie's Tax Invoices' would suggest otherwise. And in trying to understand this humiliating part of myself, I turned to the only person one should turn to when attempting to understand the innermost depths of one's psyche: Oprah.

Oprah is the god I pray to, because I'm not religious and I like to make fun of myself as an insufferable, clueless white lady who is convinced that Oprah has all the answers. The kind of lady who reads *Eat Pray Love* and puts on activewear to pick up her kids from 'self brand development class' and/or 'past-life soul therapy'. Don't get me wrong; I think Oprah probably does have all the answers. I also think it's funny for a billionaire to say that you can 'manifest' anything into your life, when manifesting for her would simply mean buying the thing she would like to manifest. (Although… what if Oprah manifested the things she wanted by *becoming* a billionaire? Whoa. Maybe she is just actually the greatest manifester of all time? Ignore my doubts. She is a holy genius.) Also, I just love her because I watch TV and think I'm important and she's on TV and tells me I'm important.

When I approached my humiliating flaw the way I imagined Oprah would, it forced me to self-reflect, and imagine my problem as an inspirational Instagram quote on a nature background. That's when I had a rare moment of profound sincerity.

I'm not looking forward to my wedding day; I'm looking forward to the days that come after the wedding day. I'm looking forward to having a partner who I love and who loves me and who thinks I'm funny. I'm looking forward to having little babies who I can teach to play the Super Nintendo that I will never throw out. I'm looking forward to putting the kids to bed and curling up with a glass of wine with a person who makes me laugh. I'm basically looking forward to being able to create the family that I never had. A family that feels secure and stays in one place and doesn't end with screaming and police and foster homes and anxiety. I would really, really just like to find someone who feels like home.

And to me, in the sad, cliché 'had a tough childhood' part of my brain, my wedding day symbolises the official start of all that, and that's why I have a folder on my computer that is so intense in its level of embarrassment, I would actually rather be caught doing a microwave popcorn foot tampon sex thing than have anyone ever open it.

I'm not about to settle though, as much as I would love to find love. I immediately delete people on Tinder who have the words 'gym' or 'Big Bang Theory' in their bio. I once broke up with a guy who tried to mansplain to me the best and safest way for women to give birth ('at home, no drugs' – I wish the future mother of his children the best of luck while she haemorrhages on the couch because she was forced to give birth like she was living in an isolated farm town from the 16th century).

I can't wait to find the person who is my home, but I'm not going to latch on to whatever person wants the job. I've tried that before, and it is empirically proven to always end with me sending embarrassing, desperate texts while having a drunken meltdown. I've thrown my phone across the room in morning-after horror enough times to know: it's better to be single than to settle with the wrong person. Get to the place where you *want* to find love, but don't *need* to find it. It'll save you from feeling like you have to be patient with the guy who says that expecting him to message back within twenty-four hours is 'too much pressure'.

My time as a single lady helped me figure out what my non-negotiables are when it comes to the kind of partner I would like to find. Non-negotiables like the following:

1. Are you okay with the fact that I don't know how to cook and I have no intention of learning how to cook?
2. Do you promise not to question me when I insist 'the dishes need to soak'?

3. Will you also then accept that 'the dishes need to soak' is code for 'I would like you to do the dishes'?

4. Are you capable of putting the toilet roll on the toilet roll holder and not just on top of the toilet? Because I'm not and we're not savages.

5. What are your thoughts on vacuuming? My thoughts are that I hope the person I love doesn't mind doing it.

6. Are you comfortable not questioning my decision to watch fourteen hours of television on a Saturday, and do you promise not to ever say to me, 'But it's a beautiful day outside!'?

7. Can you accept that each pile of clothes you see on top of places like the treadmill and my desk is actually part of a complex wardrobe system that only I understand?

8. Do you acknowledge that my taste in television is the superior taste and we will therefore watch only what I deem worthy?

9. Do you accept my flawless theory that towels don't need washing because you are already clean when you get out of the shower?

10. Can you make computers work? Because I don't understand them, except for their television streaming capabilities. And memes.

Basically my non-negotiables involve me not doing housework and getting to watch whatever TV I want, so it seems I may just be looking for a tech-savvy maid.

Oh, and I also have one other really major one that I cannot compromise on. I figured it out during my years spent in relationships, and I now know, for both my mental and physical comfort, that this non-negotiable is essential:

I need to be able to fart in front of my boyfriends.

I just do.

In fact, I consider it a sign of true love. If you can find someone who makes you feel comfortable enough to let rip at will, then you, my friend, have found a love for the ages. Don't ever let it go.

I once had a boyfriend who refused to acknowledge that women have any kind of bowel function, gas or otherwise. The idea of anything other than a perfumed stream of glitter piss coming out of me when I sat on the toilet was abhorrent to him. Actually, I think the fact there was a toilet in my house at all made him uncomfortable.

But farting was his major kryptonite. He couldn't handle any kind of air coming out of a female's bum – and it stressed me out so much I ended up with a serious and legitimate case of fart poisoning (an obviously real condition afflicting women with judgemental partners all over the world).

I discovered his phobia one night when the two of us were sitting in bed watching TV together and an involuntary fart burst out of me before I could stop it. I thought it was kind of a cute fart, to be honest. It certainly wasn't one of those suspicious ones that make you worry about a person. There's no way it could be considered close to 'shart' territory, let's put it that way.

Just a little pop that I wasn't expecting, which I didn't think twice about and immediately laughed off.

My boyfriend did not share my nonchalance about the situation.

His whole body went rigid. His head slowly and dramatically turned towards me, a look of disgust on his face that should really be reserved for somebody who just got busted doing a microwave popcorn foot tampon sex thing.

'What?' I asked, a little taken aback.

My question was met with horrified silence.

He turned his head away from me (still slowly, still dramatically), and sat for a moment, staring straight ahead, in what appeared to be disbelief. Then he snapped into action. He got out of bed and, without saying a word, walked to the bathroom and washed his hands. HE WASHED HIS HANDS. Because I farted.

He barely spoke to me for the rest of the night. I've never been so ashamed of something coming out of my body – and I once drunkenly puked up the first half of a kebab while I was still eating the second half. And I finished the second half.

From that point on, I was too petrified to ever fart in front of him, which obviously meant I was then desperate to do it all the time.

You know when you promise yourself you're not going to eat sugar, and after forty-eight hours you've become so obsessed with sugar that you end up at a convenience store at 3am, pouring Skittles into a pink and green slushie? That was me, but with farts.

I became obsessed with farting.

I came up with a secret system, where I would hold it all in until I was sure he was asleep. Then I would reach down under the covers and spread my bum cheeks, so that the air could flow out without making any noise. It kind of sounded like a breathy, elegant 'puh'. Sort of how you imagine Kate Middleton would fart.

The only problem was, once I had silently let the farts out, there was nowhere for them to go. I had to keep them trapped under the covers for fear the smell would wake him up. And if one little pop made him wash his hands, I assumed twelve farts trapped under the doona would lead to some kind of heavy-duty hose-down situation in the front yard.

So there I was, for months and months, waiting for him to fall asleep so I could spread my cheeks and set silent gas-balls free into the universe. Even in the middle of summer, I would keep the doona tightly clamped around my body – a bizarre little Dutch oven sweat lodge of shame.

The plan's one fatal flaw was revealed when he woke up one night and lifted the doona. I can't imagine what it would have been like to be hit right in the face with that epic wall of gas. I think I saw tears in his eyes.

He slept on the couch.

After that, secret systems were out. If I was ever going to fart, just to be safe, it needed to be when he wasn't within a ten-kilometre radius of my current location.

I knew the relationship was doomed when I started to choose farting over him. Some nights I would avoid sleepovers just so I could stay home on my own and fart in peace. Without all the guilt. Without all his *looks*.

I was essentially picking farts over orgasms. It was never going to work.

So that's what I need I suppose: a tech-savvy maid who understands that women sometimes need to fart. What a dream.

And if I ever find someone like that, I definitely don't have a wedding planned and ready to go, because there's definitely no folder on my computer with wedding stuff in it. Just 'Rosie's Tax Invoices'.

And probably some weird porn, because I totally googled 'microwave popcorn foot tampon sex thing'.

'Jacob,' I said. 'Jacob!'

He was sleeping in a chair next to my hospital bed, having taken over from my friend Jamila, who had spent the first night with me.

'Jacob!'

'What? What's wrong?' he asked, pulling his eye mask off. He had bought it for me, but since I had brilliantly taken caffeine tablets in my attempt to sleep forever, the eye mask wasn't exactly going to make a difference.

'Have you noticed,' I said, 'that all the nurses here have really awesome Nikes?'

The curtains were pulled around my bed, so all I'd been staring at for the last two hours were people's shoes. My nausea was unbearable – the doctor said that was partly the pills, partly the vodka, and partly the drip I was now on to try and protect my liver. Not only was I exhausted, but I also wanted to sleep just to get some relief from the constant need to vomit. But sleep wasn't going to happen, so I had been focussing on the shoes.

'What?' Jacob asked.

'The nurses,' I said. 'It's like they're sponsored by Nike! All their shoes are so cool. I'm fairly certain there's a social hierarchy here based on the shoes. The nurse who seems the coolest has the best ones, and nobody talks to the girl who's wearing Crocs. I think she's a social outcast. It's not nice. I want to buy her a pair of Nikes. Do you think I should get a pair of Nikes? I do need a new pair of sneakers, and obviously Nikes are where it's at. I've seen, like, four pairs here that I want to buy. Also, you can tell who the doctors are because they don't wear sneakers. The doctors are the ones with nice shoes. Heels. I bet the nurses just look at them in their fancy heeled boots and think, "Yeah, that'd be nice," like, shoes with heels is the ultimate sign that you're not on your feet for eight hours straight, like the snobs, you know what I mean? Like, you can be the queen-bee nurse with the coolest Nikes, but you're still not good enough for the snobby heels doctor group.'

Jacob just stared at me. 'What?'

He was still recovering from the enema poo blast. We had both seen it hit the other side of the curtain and splash on to the floor. Jacob was horrified, but sitting behind me, he wasn't sure if I had seen it at first, and he didn't want to add to my nausea by telling me about it. So I just lay there, with my back to him, listening as the horrors of the enema poo unfolded, and he sat behind me, doing the same, neither of us realising the other was witnessing the nightmare also.

Someone soon came and mopped up the … *mess* that was on the floor. But nobody did anything about the mess on the curtain.

I lay there, waiting, thinking someone was going to come and fix it. Probably men in hazmat suits, who would rip the curtain down, lock it in a cement barrel and dump it wherever governments illegally hide toxic waste. The kind of place where the three-eyed fish from *The Simpsons* would come from. But nobody ever came. After about fifteen minutes, I turned around and saw Jacob just staring at the curtain in horror.

'Holy Oprah. Do you think anyone is going to clean that?' I asked.

'I thought you were asleep!' he said. 'Were you awake for it? You were awake during the ... *event*?'

'Dude. I was watching the whole thing. If that curtain wasn't pulled across, it would have sprayed all over us.'

He laughed. I wanted to, but the nausea was too much.

'Seriously though,' he said. 'The curtain. They better be sending someone to get rid of the fucking curtain.'

Hours had gone by since that conversation, and while I was now focussed on the nurses' Nikes, Jacob was still fixated on the curtain. Which, by the way, still had shit sprayed all over it. The man who'd had the enema was now gone, but his shit remained.

I have never been the ringleader of a major crime operation.
(I was. For one glorious month, I was.)

It started small. A Kit Kat here. A sausage roll there. And it seemed so harmless at first; just a bit of cheeky fun. Then my ambition and greed revealed a seedy high-school underbelly that I did not have the nerves to handle. It only took four weeks for me to realise that I was not built for a life of sophisticated crime. Channel Nine was never going to make a highly rated TV miniseries about me (in which Rhonda from those insurance ads plays every female character, with a special cameo by Sam Neill to add gravitas). It turns out I was not destined to go down in Australian history as a glamorous Queen of Crime. But for one nail-biting month, I did make it to the very top of the ladder.

At thirteen, I was a 'canteen prefect', which is really just a fancy way of saying 'I am an unpaid canteen worker because the school cannot afford to make this a salaried job'.

Basically, a few other students and I worked alongside parent volunteers at the canteen counter. It wasn't a glamorous job, but it *was* one that provided you with a free lunch valued up to five dollars every time you did it, which in my case tended to be once or twice a week. I realised pretty quickly though, enterprising young lady that I was, that food and drink up to the value of five dollars was actually a pretty shitty deal, considering I was giving up my entire lunch hour to earn it. I would much rather have been sitting on the side of the oval, reading *Dolly* magazine and pretending to laugh at the questions other teenage girls had submitted to Dolly Doctor. (I say 'pretending' to laugh because obviously I did what every other girl my age did: acted like the column was stupid while in public, then rushed home to devour it in private, because I had also wondered if that ingrown hair on my labia meant I was somehow pregnant with triplets. Even though I'd never had a period, let alone sex, I was still convinced I was going to end up on one of those TV specials about the clueless girl who thought she was just a bit constipated and unexpectedly gives birth forty-five minutes later.)

The first couple of times I worked as a canteen prefect, I followed the rules and took people's money and gave them their lunch of Fanta and Mars Bars, and everything was above board. Then, it dawned on me: why would I put the money in the cash register (which was literally just a shoebox in front of me) when I could put the money in my pocket instead? There were a couple of mums working on the canteen counter, along with a couple of students like me, and we each had our own high-tech shoebox cash register. But there was never more than five or six of us in total, and we had to serve a school with two thousand students who all wanted their meat pies and Wagon Wheels at the same time. It was more chaotic than any retail job I would go on to have in my university years. Working on the high-school canteen counter was like *The Hunger Games* mixed with *Fight Club* mixed with Boxing Day sales. Everyone was just trying to survive and nobody noticed what the hell anybody else was doing. Putting some sneaky change into my pocket would've been easy.

But I was smart. I was organised. I was first in my grade in most of my subjects, and I spent my weekends doing homework and preparing for next week's classes while reading history books that my mum had specially ordered for me. I was an insufferable overachiever (this was before I realised how much easier school is when you're lazy), and if I was going to start pocketing sneaky cash while on canteen duty, there was no way I was going to half-arse it. I wasn't just going to brazenly take money out of the shoebox cash register – I needed a system that would bring maximum profits but also gave me deniability should I get caught doing anything dodgy. Basically, I needed to create a profitable yet perfect crime. One in which I would make lots of money but never get caught.

I cannot even tell you how much of a genius I thought I was for realising this. How nobody had yet managed to revolutionise theft in this way was beyond me. *Steal* stuff, but *don't* get caught! It was clearly very simple as far as I was concerned. Anybody who'd ever been arrested was an idiot.

Now, this was 1999, before everyone was allergic to gluten, nuts and sugar, so we supplied pretty standard Aussie school-lunch foods of the day: everything from meat pies and Zooper Doopers to chicken nuggets and wedges. All the colours on the fizzy drink spectrum, every chocolate bar and chip flavour known to man, and of course: Bubble o' Bills. There was also usually some sad-looking homemade sandwiches covered in some even sadder-looking plastic wrap, but the overzealous parent volunteer who made those generally figured out pretty fast not to bother. Who's going to buy egg salad on multigrain when they can have a Chiko Roll?

And kids *really* wanted to eat this stuff back then (I still do, to be honest). There was no shortage of students wrestling to get to the front of the canteen line. There was also no shortage of students who tried to wrangle freebies out of me, and *that* is where I saw my in.

I developed a system. I knew people wanted free stuff and I knew I wanted cash. I also knew that I had access to the free stuff and the cash. So, I made sure word slowly spread around to a few select individuals that if they came to me at the counter, they could give me a couple of dollars, order whatever they wanted (always valued at far, far more than a couple of dollars), and I would then give them everything they asked for and put their measly few coins in the shoebox. BUT (and here's the genius part), I would also give them a huge amount of 'change', usually about ten bucks. Then, after lunch, as a fee for hooking them up, I would go and collect eighty per cent of the cash I had given them. So they got their money back, plus a massive lunch, and I pocketed at least $8.00 per person.

This system meant that I wasn't just brazenly taking money out of the shoebox and putting it in my pocket, which I was terrified would be noticed. I was taking people's money, giving them food, then giving them change, which was exactly my job description. If the adult volunteers in charge ever looked up from their own shoeboxes and over at me to see what I was doing, everything would look completely normal. Just Rosie the good girl selflessly giving up her lunch hour as a canteen prefect.

Then I'd collect my dirty money and me and my friends would go to the shops after school and make it rain with endless chips and gravy. THE PERFECT CRIME.

I made sure to keep things very small at first. I assumed that if I kept the dollar amount low, nothing would ever be noticed. It's not like there was any kind of inventory in this place – money was literally just thrown into a shoebox in exchange for junk food. The only way I would seem suspicious is if I handed in an empty box at the end of lunch. So I had about five people working for me. All friends who could be trusted. Collecting between eight and ten bucks from each of them meant I would get close to $50 every time I worked in the canteen. I was thirteen. I might as well have been a millionaire.

To me, it felt like a victimless crime. Never mind that the school often didn't have enough chairs in classrooms and an entire building riddled with asbestos became an abandoned place kids hooked up in because the school couldn't afford to knock it down – I felt like I was taking from a wealthy corporation that surely didn't need the money anyway. In fact, my taking money from them was probably a *moral act*, since I was spending it on far more worthy causes than them, with all their questioning whether evolution was a thing and making me participate in team sports. I was like Robin Hood, taking from the rich and giving to the poor (me), so I could spend the money on what the community desperately needed (food for my friends and other stuff that I really wanted for me).

Also, at that stage, I just didn't really feel like I owed the world anything. My dad had killed himself. My mum was an alcoholic. I kept getting shipped around to live with different people who weren't that thrilled to have me there. I was in Year 8 and had already been to at least eleven schools. I never knew what horror show was waiting for me when I got home. The world owed *me*, not the other way around. Adults had been letting me down my entire life – taking some of their money was just my way of making sure I was being compensated for everything they'd put me through.

But (luckily, I think, for the world at large, since I was clearly on my way to masterminding much larger *Ocean's 11*-style crimes) fear and anxiety started to get the better of me as the scale of my canteen operation grew. I've often thought that's the reason I never ended up living a life on the wrong side of the law, like so many other people who grew up with childhoods similar to mine. Given this early foray into shoebox coin theft, it seems I could have easily gone that way. But I didn't feel guilt about the stealing; I was just a total coward. Breaking rules terrifies me, and I figured that out about two weeks into my life as a criminal.

And even though I quickly went back to the right side of the law because I was scared and not because I felt like I was doing anything wrong, I still completely understand the logic behind behaving badly because you feel like the world hasn't done you any favours. If all anybody's ever done is let you down, and you can find an easier (usually illegal) way to get something that you want or need, why shouldn't you take it? Why wouldn't you take the easier way when your life has been so damn hard already? Can anyone really blame you for that?

I grappled with those thoughts at thirteen, and I'd really like to say that I internally debated privilege and moral relativism and came to the conclusion that the world doesn't owe you anything no matter how crappy a hand you've been dealt, and that you aren't entitled to behave how you please just because you've built up some level of cosmic debt via a crappy childhood.

I would *like* to say I had those thoughts, but I was not even close to being that smart at the time. (To be honest, I'm not entirely certain I really understand what 'moral relativism' means today, but now I can say I discussed it in one of my books and damn it if that doesn't sound impressive.)

I didn't decide to bring my crime ring to an end because I thought it was wrong, I decided to bring it to an end because I was scared shitless.

Word spreads fast in high school − about as fast as hashtags spread today when somebody is being shamed by people on Twitter − and word of the dweeby girl who could hook you up at the canteen counter was fast becoming legend. I'd like to say it was my fault, but this one can only be blamed on my vagina. That hussy.

A cute boy who I had a massive crush on, and who would never have talked to me otherwise, came to my line at the canteen one day, which had suspiciously grown a lot longer than the other lines. He told me what he wanted. I gave it to him. He gave me his money. I gave him his change. Then he just stood there.

'Oh,' he said, looking down at his pie (and sauce that I'd charged him ten cents extra for because when I wasn't partaking in grand theft I was actually a stickler for the rules).

'What?' I said, momentarily snapped out of the trance his face had me under.

'Well, it's just that I thought that, you know, you gave out like ... *free stuff.*'

My eyes widened. 'What! No!' I said, laughing in an exaggerated manner for the FBI cameras that I was sure were planted all over the canteen. (Yes – I am fully aware we don't have the FBI in Australia, but I was raised on television. I probably would have called 911 in an emergency and died as I waited for an ambulance that never came.)

I leaned in close to him. 'Not so loud,' I said, feeling all kinds of tingles in my special place now that we were practically touching noses. 'Okay. Just this once. What do you actually want?'

'Um, shit. Um ...'

'HURRY THE FUCK UP,' I whispered urgently, like we were robbing a bank and he was fumbling with the getaway bag.

'Okay, okay. A Coke. A chocolate donut. Two rainbow Paddle Pops. And ... ummm ... FUCK. Just give me another pie.'

I collected the items in question and put them on the counter in front of him.

'Now,' I said. 'Very casually and normally take some money from your wallet and give it to me.'

He seemed perplexed. 'But I don't get it. I thought it was meant to be fr—'

'JUST GIVE ME SOME FUCKING COINS.'

He handed me a couple of dollars. I gave him back three five-dollar notes. He looked adorably confused and the whole exchange was giving me bean tingles.

'Keep that and meet me in English after lunch,' I said, as I called the next person in the line.

I met him later to get my cut and explain the system. It then, bless his good-looking yet simple heart, took less than twenty-four hours for several more students to know about the system. Shit. I knew better than to just bend the rules for someone like that, even someone to whom I had thought about giving a blow job (a thing I had heard about that I assumed just involved blowing on a person's penis, not unlike blowing out the candles on a birthday cake).

I had broken the cone of silence because I wanted to blow out this boy's penis candle. Damn my vagina and her power over my brain.

My canteen line continued to grow much longer than any other – comically so. Business was booming, but it made me nervous. Everywhere in school I went, I was getting sly winks and pats on the back, but I couldn't shake the feeling that a

SWAT team was going to descend on me at any moment, brandishing warrants to search my locker and holding up photos of me buying chips and gravy and lip gloss and magazines — my lavish lifestyle clear evidence of my crimes.

I decided that the next week I was refusing all illegitimate service. I needed to lay low for a while and reassess my priorities, maybe even the whole system itself. I just wasn't built for the kind of heat I had created. The fear of getting caught was too much; every day was filled with an anxious dread that not even the latest NSYNC album could snap me out of. I couldn't go to prison without knowing what it was like to have an actual living boy make contact with my vagina, rather than just simulating the feeling by humping my mattress. I still had so much to live for.

I lasted one more shift on the canteen counter before I completely retired as prefect. Those close to me with inside knowledge of the system thought I was crazy to give it up, and I'm sure some other group of kids immediately took over and started living the high life. But I never regretted my decision to walk away. From the day I handed in my shoebox for the last time, I felt nothing but relief. My life had been filled with anxiety from the moment I was born, and I was not about to do anything to add to it.

So, do I feel guilty *now*, or am I just a total psychopath who would be breaking laws left, right and centre if not for her crippling fear of getting caught? Well, honestly, it did take me a while to feel like the world didn't owe me something for giving me two alcoholic parents. It does take a person some time to stop being pissed off about that. But luckily, because my fear stopped me from committing any more major crimes, my moral compass was able to develop as normal. So, yes, I do feel bad about briefly being the ringleader of a major crime operation. I did not go on to rob convenience stores because of my crappy childhood. I may have ended up with PTSD, but I have not robbed a 7-Eleven. You're welcome, society.

(And no, that cute but simple boy who told everyone about the system never made contact with my vagina. He blew my cover, but not me. Crime really doesn't pay.)

Hey mon frère with your derrière something something cush.

    'She's going to need to be on the drip for at least sixteen hours.'

    Something something da da da it's Jack's Subway Tush.

    'Do you know how many she took?'

    I really need it it's Jack's Subway tush.

    'Jacob's on his way.'

    Something something it's —

    'Hopefully she'll sleep.'

    Jaaaaaaaack's Suuuubwaaaay Tuuuuuush.

    I did not sleep. Here's a little tip: if despair has taken over your body, is pushing nothing but darkness through your veins and all you want to do is sleep and never wake up, make sure you don't take pills with caffeine in them. Taking pills with caffeine in them will, in fact, have the opposite effect – they will cause you to stay awake and never sleep. And your despair will still be there, pushing darkness through your veins. It'll just be laughing at you now as well.

I took the pills to make me sleep forever, and they were specifically designed to keep me awake. I could not believe the hilarious irony of my screw-up.

They were paracetamol pills, but the box said they were 'EXTRA', which I took to mean 'extra strong'. Like, really hardcore paracetamol, filled with lots of codeine. I don't know why I assumed that. I didn't read the box properly, I suppose. I had bought them at Abu Dhabi airport the week before, on a stopover during the almost 24-hour journey from London to Melbourne. I was recovering from gastro, was dehydrated, exhausted, and a few days away from having actual hallucinations. So, not exactly in the right mindset to be comprehending the medical labels on boxes of tablets. When I found the 'EXTRA' paracetamol in the intense-looking red box in Abu Dhabi, I figured they would have a magic effect, not unlike heroin and general anaesthetic, mixed together with the feeling I get after falling into a food coma from gorging on pasta. Basically I figured if I took a couple, they would knock me out for the entire second leg of my trip.

I did not sleep at all on the second leg of that trip. It turns out, the 'EXTRA' magic ingredient in the paracetamol is not actually codeine but caffeine, designed for people who need to take something for a headache without feeling drowsy. Despite this being clearly labelled on the box, it had eluded me.

And it was still eluding me a few days later when I took every single pill left in that clearly labelled box. Pills I took after drinking a lot of vodka just to be sure.

So there I was, lying in a hospital bed, about to be awake for the next forty painful hours. Forced to keep singing that stupid *Will & Grace* song that I couldn't remember the words to, forced to look at the poo-stained curtain next to me, and forced to think about why there was so much darkness in my veins that my mind had collapsed in on itself, ending in a complete nervous breakdown.

Forced to think about Tony.

It was strange not having him in the ER with me then. He had been standing next to me both times I had woken up in hospital as an adult. 'Hey, crazy lady,' he had said, when I woke up after my PTSD had led to me being hospitalised in my early twenties.

'You already look skinny!' was his opening line when I opened my eyes after weight-loss surgery at twenty-seven. 'Do you remember your name, skinny lady?'

I looked directly into the phone camera he had shoved in my face. 'Oprah,' I replied, my voice filled with conviction and sincerity. 'I am Oprah.'

Both times, we had burst into laughter, because that was us: we laughed and laughed and laughed and laughed. Usually at our own expense.

I met Tony on the first day of drama school in 2005. Antonio Sergi was an adorable Italian boy from Griffith, a country town about eight hours' drive from Sydney. He dressed like he had just stepped off the soundstage of a teen-drama set in the fashion world. Everybody would laugh at the latest ridiculous thing he was wearing, but would be rushing out to buy it just a couple of months later, when Tony had already moved on. He had a trucker hat (very cool at the time, okay?) emblazoned with his nickname, T-BUFF, which had come about in Griffith because of his obsession with *Buffy the Vampire Slayer*. He was early 2000s youth culture personified, and we clicked instantly.

Tony was fresh out of high school, and I had just dropped out of my first year at Sydney University, when we both ended up at the Australian Academy of Dramatic Art. We were both eighteen, both obsessed with comedy and already reading this new thing called a 'blog' by Perez Hilton, while everybody else devoured Chekhov and Ibsen. Tony didn't take life, or acting, too seriously, which is why we got along so well. Along with a few others in our year, we were more interested in recreating sketches from *Saturday Night Live* than we were in rehearsing a traditional soliloquy. But it didn't matter; drama school tends to be a catchall for young people who know they love being creative, who know they love to perform or write or design or direct, but have no idea how to approach that. Drama school is the safety net that catches the kids who just couldn't balance on the traditional education tightrope. Some wanted to be Shakespearian actors, others wanted to imitate Tina Fey in *Weekend Update*. We all ended up together.

I had left university disillusioned and confused about what I actually wanted to do, and I figured since I'd always loved acting and writing, drama school might be a good place to figure out a plan. I kind of floated into it, hoping it would work out. Tony, on the other hand, was completely clear about where he was supposed to be. Famous in his country town for being a born comedian and performer, he was the one who everybody knew was going to 'get out'. I didn't realise at the time how huge a deal it was that Tony came to Sydney by himself, looking to build a life away from everything he had ever known. Especially when his massive Italian family in Griffith was already a pretty great ready-made life. All the parents had gone to school together, married, had children, watched them grow up at the same time, and now those children, Tony's generation, were about to repeat the cycle, by getting married and soon raising children of their own. All going to the same schools, same shops, same church. Tony's entire life had been spent in the warm embrace of family and familiarity, something that, with my tumultuous childhood, I couldn't believe he had walked away from. It wasn't easy for him, especially as he got older, being away from his best friends and family, watching from another city as his generation of Griffith kids grew into adults together. But he knew what he was passionate about, he knew what he wanted to do, and he knew that meant leaving a wonderful life in his hometown. Tony always knew he was too big for Griffith.

From the first day we met, in that crappy drama-school common room, in that crappy building on that crappy street in Sydney, Tony was holding my hand through life. When I met Tony I was struggling with PTSD. After a childhood filled with abuse and neglect, a father who'd died and a mother who'd left my sisters and me as wards of the state, I'd ended up in a boarding school where I was bullied to breaking point, followed by a university where I'd felt confused and alone. By the time I landed at drama school, I was only just beginning to climb out of the hole I'd been hiding in. Tony took my hand and never let it go.

He started by convincing me I was funny, and introduced me to all the female comedians he idolised that I'd never heard of. We'd watch Chelsea Handler, Kathy Griffin, Wanda Sykes, Miranda Hart, Mo'Nique, Sarah Silverman ... 'You could do that, Ro,' he'd say, more sure of me than I ever was.

When I was playing the role of Jan in *Grease the Musical*, the only time I ever fumbled my lines was the day Tony was in the audience for the first time, because the second I walked out onstage he started cheering and laughing hysterically before I'd even said anything. Afterwards, when I asked him about that premature laugh, he just said, 'Because I knew you were going to nail it.'

In our last year of drama school, when the uncle I'd been living with asked me to move out, Tony welcomed me into his apartment, no questions asked. We went on to live together, on and off, for ten years. Sometimes heading in different directions to do other things, but always landing back with each other.

We grew into adults together, something I couldn't have done without Tony by my side. He comforted me after every break-up. He laughed with me through every drunken mishap. He understood my mental health and never judged me for it. He was one of the few friends I introduced to my mother, while she sat drunk and alone in a room filled with empty wine boxes.

Tony was there as jobs came and went, relationships came and went, weight came and went. He witnessed my complete physical transformation: when he met me at drama school, I weighed sixty kilograms. He cried with me as an eating disorder saw that number rise to one hundred and fifty, and he supported me when I had most of my stomach removed to try and get back to a body that I recognised.

From the moment I met Tony at eighteen, he was my North Star. He was the person I looked to when I felt lost. He was the person who would drop everything to be by my side. He was my soulmate.

I'd like to think I was the same to him, but I can't say that I was. Not because I didn't try to be, or because our relationship was one-sided, but because Tony was just so generous with his time, his love and his friendship. He was silly and hilarious and loved *Real Housewives* and sketch comedy and fashion and *People* magazine (which he ordered from America because celebrity gossip is serious). But those were just the superficial parts of Tony: the parts that made him fun to drink wine with and watch TV with. What was actually most striking about Tony was his ability to make everyone he knew feel like they were the most important person in his life. Tony may have been *my* soulmate, but he had at least thirty-five other soulmates that he was keeping track of. Every person in his life relied on Tony for love and support, and the fact that he was able to give it to all of them without question was his true gift as a human being. Tony may have always been holding my hand, but he was also holding the hands of many others. He was everybody's North Star.

A few years out of drama school, Tony and I were living in a tiny apartment in Newtown, just west of the city. We had no money, and besides a bed and a TV each (of course), no furniture. For the first six months we lived there, we used a blow-up mattress instead of a couch, with one of us constantly having to cover the holes that all the air would leak out of. We'd usually get through about three episodes of *Honey Boo Boo* before the mattress would be flat and on the floor. Then we'd spend half an hour pumping it back up again, before waiting for it to slowly deflate, laughing like banshees as we sunk into each other. We'd head up to King Street at about 10pm, because we knew that's when Clem's Chicken Shop would be wanting to get rid of stuff at the end of the night, so we'd order a few measly bits of chicken and then Tony would charm them into giving us free chips and salad. We also figured out that the 7-Eleven had new Krispy Kreme donuts delivered just after midnight, so if we went in just before that we'd usually manage to get all the leftovers from the day. 'Just here to buy a can of drink,' we'd say loudly, while looking longingly at the donuts. Whether it was pity or admiration at our sass I'm not sure, but the 7-Eleven guy always gave us the donuts.

Neither of us had ended up where we wanted to after drama school, me in particular. Tony had travelled a bit, lived in Melbourne for a while, went to auditions and tried to get an agent. I had gone to university and finished a degree in creative writing, which meant, combined with drama school, I had studied for six years and was basically only qualified to work in a coffee shop or a call centre.

I ended up in a call centre. My weight gain meant I had no chance of getting any acting auditions, so I hadn't even bothered. My writing degree was ... not exactly vocational in its approach. I learned a lot about beat poetry and not so much about how to, you know, get a job. (Our assignments were often of the 'just do whatever you *feel*' variety. I once googled 'synonyms for vagina', then copy-and-pasted thirty of them into the centre of a single page, wrote some crap about it being a comment on feminism in literature, and walked away with a High Distinction. I did the whole thing the night before it was due, while laughing hysterically over a box of wine. It was probably the highlight of my entire degree.)

When Tony and I moved into that little apartment in Newtown, I was lost again, just like when we'd first met at drama school. I'd go into work, answer calls on a switchboard (usually just hanging up on people, if I'm being perfectly honest), come home, go into my room and watch TV. Tony could see I was in a hole, and he decided to jump in, stick his hands under my bum and help boost me out of it.

Once again having more faith in me than I had in myself, he reminded me that he thought I was brilliant and talented and funny, and it didn't matter that I didn't think I was, because he did. He encouraged me to contribute my first article to an online website, and when it was picked up and published, he jumped around the house screaming for a solid ten minutes. Then he took me out for champagne to celebrate, and told me that it was time I started a blog and a Twitter account, because 'everything these days is about brand-building'. At that stage, I barely used my computer for anything other than Facebook and Google, but Tony always just had an innate understanding of what was next.

He helped me build a website (Tony-approved branding: ROSIEWATERLAND.COM) and sat and listened as I read every new story I wrote to him, on the blow-up mattress/couch. He laughed hysterically at every word, which may seem indulgent, but I think he just knew that I really needed it.

After a lifetime of struggle and disappointment, I was so broken and scared to do anything, and he knew that I needed him to walk me through becoming a writer in the tiniest of baby steps. Laughing at my jokes. Fawning over everything I wrote. Crying with joy every time I got something published. All of that had the most profound effect on me. He was pulling me out of my hole and pushing me into the spotlight, whether I liked it or not.

When my writing started to build a fan base, and my articles were getting published more and more often, Tony would obsess for days over what he could do to get me even further 'out there'. He would tweet things like 'Justin Bieber and Selena Gomez BREAK UP? Read the details here!' Then he provided a link to the latest story on my blog. One night my website got so many hits it crashed. 'Now you can tell people that your blog has amazing numbers,' Tony said, laughing. He bought a chalkboard, hung it up in the living room and would write the blog's numbers on there every day. I'd get home from the call centre and see '50,000 HITS!!! CONGRATULATIONS ROSIE

YOU GENIUS!' the second I walked in the door. The day Mamamia, Australia's largest women's website, offered me a full-time writing position, he burst into tears.

I thought I was doomed to work in that call centre forever, and I escaped it because of him. Every word I wrote, I wrote with his encouragement. Nobody supported or was more invested in my success than him.

And his support had no limits.

When I started at Mamamia, I was petrified. Petrified of everything. Of meeting new people, of being in an office where I had to socialise, of everybody discovering that my writing was actually terrible. Tony had to push me out the door every morning (always in an outfit he had chosen). When the editorial team would go out for drinks or dinner, he would come with me, as my social safety blanket, so I wouldn't be crippled with shyness. If, as I quickly realised was inevitable when you write online, I was attacked on social media for an article I'd written, he was the first person on Twitter, blasting people for going after me and tweeting links to every piece I'd ever written, just to prove how brilliant he thought I was. He would log in to my Twitter and Facebook accounts for me, and delete nasty comments before I could see them and fall into a guaranteed despair spiral.

The very first time I did radio, Tony came with me to the studio and waited in the greenroom. Same with the first time I appeared on television. When my profile really started to take off, he was with me every step of the way. My followers reached into the thousands, then the tens of thousands, then over a hundred thousand, and where I felt afraid and unworthy, he never doubted that I deserved my success. He screamed and cried with me on the phone when I was offered a book deal, and he was the one to proudly sign the contract as a witness.

The book tour terrified me: the idea of having to meet people I didn't know and talk to them and be 'on' and impress everyone who had come to see me. So Tony came to every single tour stop. It was eventually just assumed by my publishers that they would need to plan for two people whenever and wherever I was doing an event. We jokingly referred to Tony as my 'Executive Brand Manager', a fancy title he could put on his resume, since he had stopped working just to support me emotionally while my career soared.

I was asked if I wanted to write and tour a comedy show, and just a couple of years after rushing home from a call centre so I could hide in my room, just a couple of years after being confused and lost and feeling worthless, I said yes. I said yes to standing onstage by myself for an hour, entertaining people with stories I had written.

Tony listened to me rehearse in my bedroom, pointing a lamp in my direction so I could get used to the spotlight. Of course, he came to every show.

By that stage, the blow-up mattress was long gone. We had moved into a much nicer apartment and I had bought an actual couch. I was even making enough money that we could just buy Krispy Kremes and not try to scam freebies from the exhausted 7-Eleven guy. And it was all because of Tony. I may have written the words that people liked to read (much to my disbelief), but I would never have been able to write them in the first place if Tony hadn't been there with me, pushing me, encouraging me, every step of the way.

After my comedy show, Tony decided to go to Austin, Texas, for a while. He had studied there for a semester completing his Masters degree in Media Arts and Production, and wanted to spend some time with the friends he had made there. It was perfect timing for us both, really; I had been offered the chance to develop my own TV show in Melbourne, so Tony leaving Sydney for a while felt like the perfect time for me to leave too. We decided that I'd move to Melbourne and get set up in an apartment while he went to Austin. When it was time to work on the show, he'd come back, move in with me, and we'd go on to win a million Emmys together. I couldn't imagine making a show without him, not just because I needed him to hold my hand, but also because he was just so brilliant, both comically and creatively. He was probably the only person I knew who had more of an instinct for television than I did. It was our dream job, and we were going to do it together.

I hated moving to Melbourne on my own. Hated it. Not only was it the first time I'd been without Tony in a long time, but I was in a new state and didn't have a lot of friends. Not for their lack of trying though: a lot of Melbourne people reached out to me when I first moved there. But without Tony to come with me while I socialised, my shyness meant I was too scared to go. I spent a lot of time in my apartment, only leaving for the occasional TV writing job, or to record a podcast, or to ride my bike through the park (I was trying very hard to fit in as a Melbourne hipster), but mostly I just stayed at home.

I was lonely. And I had underestimated how important the comfort and familiarity I had built for myself in Sydney was. After a childhood in which I attended more than twenty schools, lived in countless houses with different families, called more suburbs home than I could count, when I reached adulthood all I wanted was to stay in one place. And I did. I moved to Sydney's inner-west when I was twenty and I never left. Not even to travel. Of course I wanted to see the world, and watched longingly as friends my age did so, but after the life I'd lived, once I was in control of it, all I wanted to do was stay put. And while Tony and I changed apartments a few times, I had been living in and around the inner-west for almost ten years when I moved to Melbourne. I had built a secure, familiar place for myself for the first time in my life, and I did not anticipate how much I would miss that.

But, as lonely as I felt, I pushed through, because I knew Tony was coming. I knew that when he arrived and moved in with me, we were going to take Melbourne by storm. (At least he would, while I quietly waved behind him.) I knew it was going to be brilliant once Tony arrived. He had helped me choose the apartment and was already planning how he would redecorate everything.

Things would be better when Tony came. I would be braver. Melbourne was going to be brilliant once Tony was holding my hand. I just had to hold out a few more months.

When the school holidays came around, I paid for my thirteen-year-old niece Allira to fly down and stay with me for a week. I figured I'd take her out, do a bunch of fun stuff, and feel a little bit connected to home for a while. I was getting over a bout of glandular fever, which I'd picked up after making out with a 21-year-old at a party earlier that year (hint: don't make out with 21-year-olds), so I wasn't feeling great, but having Allira around really cheered me up. Then, on her second day in Melbourne, she got a stomach bug. I'd taken her to high tea (which, frankly, she didn't seem impressed enough with, considering how much I'd paid for it), and on the way home she went a very weird shade of pale. By six that night, we were both on the couch, miserable, watching TV and feeling like crap. I made her watch *The Sixth Sense*, which completely perplexed her. 'Why is it, like, fuzzy?' she asked, having never seen a film that wasn't digital. 'Is it really old or something?'

'No!' I said, offended. 'I think it came out when I was in about Year 6. So I guess maybe twenty years ago.'

'Rosie, that's old,' she said, not looking up from her phone. 'It's like the person who made it needs glasses.'

She had a point. When you watch a movie that hasn't been adapted into the crisp, clear viewing experience we've become used to, it really does feel like the quality is defective in some way. I could understand why she kept calling it 'fuzzy'.

She also found it incomprehensible. She thought the ending was dumb. (Her: 'I'm sorry, but he must have tried to buy something at some point.' Me: 'SHUT UP WITH YOUR PESKY DETAILS!')

Accepting that she was sufficiently unimpressed with my movie choice and would prefer to watch quality programming on her phone, I left her on the couch and went to bed.

I woke up late the next morning, and sat in bed, checking Facebook and Instagram as I always do before my feet even touch the ground for the day.

My head still foggy, I noticed a message from one of Tony's cousins, Josephine. I read it, but felt like my just-awake brain had mixed it up, so I read it again. My heart started to beat faster. Well that can't be right, I thought. Tony's always been a hypochondriac. There's been some mix-up, and the wrong message had made its way to Griffith. Tony had mentioned a seizure to me a couple of weeks earlier – he was probably just in hospital. I messaged Josephine back, gave her my number and asked her to call me, running past Allira on the couch and onto the balcony, which was the only place I got strong enough reception to have a phone call.

My phone rang. I answered it.

'Rosie, I'm so sorry. Tony passed away.'

I was really emotionally scarred by my abortion.
(Yeah, um, not really. Sorry.)

My face must have looked exactly how the over-achieving sperm inside me was making my stomach feel, because the nurse giving me my results didn't even take a moment to assume that this was a life event I was thrilled about.

'Oh. Um. Oh. I'm so sorry. It's positive. You're pregnant.'

When someone says 'I'm sorry' instead of 'Congratulations', you know that you are definitely too young to be pregnant.

I wanted to vomit. Not because I was terrified or shocked or anxious to find out that I was knocked up at twenty-one, but because whatever little swimmer had managed to successfully plow its way into me was now having some kind of epic sperm-gastro problem that could only be explained by it having eaten bad fish of some kind. Not only had my egg been infiltrated, it had been infiltrated by an obviously defective sperm with a stomach bug. And now all I wanted to do was vomit, all day, every day.

That's how I knew, actually. I can remember the exact moment I knew I was pregnant. I could just feel something wrong in my body.

I was working in a cinema, and got a hot flush while sitting on the toilet. Then I was really suddenly hit with a wave of nausea like nothing I had ever felt before. It was the kind of nausea that takes away any sense of dignity that a person has – I literally took off my top and bra, lay down on the cold tiles of the bathroom floor with my pants around my ankles, just praying for the feeling to pass and being absolutely certain that no other person in the history of time had ever suffered like I was suffering in that exact moment.

I spent the next ten minutes throwing up pretty violently (this wasn't 'cough a little while a boy holds your hair back' throwing up, this was heaving, 'the blood vessels in your eyes burst' kind of throwing up). It was graphic. Once I was done, I sat back on the toilet, a little worried to be honest, as I didn't know if vaginal tinea was a thing but if you're ever going to get it, it would definitely be after lying naked on the floor of a public cinema bathroom. I closed my eyes and took a deep breath, trying to compose myself. And as I sat there, entirely naked now except for my shoes, the words just flashed across my brain: YOU'RE PREGNANT.

Fuck.

I peed on a stick as soon as I finished work and the two blue lines immediately came into focus. *Immediately.* Like they were shoving the certainty in my face. They didn't even give me the decency of some ambiguity.

Fuckity fuck shitburgers.

I threw up again, because the initial vomit had clearly only been some kind of vomit-welcoming ceremony, designed to introduce me to a new, vomit-focussed way of life. And from that moment on, the vomiting did not stop. It was all day, every day. That's why I became convinced my egg had been fertilised by a defective sperm with a stomach bug. I was so nauseous I could barely stand upright. And then, a few days after peeing on that stick, I was still trying to hold in vom while sitting opposite the very concerned-looking nurse who had just taken my blood.

'This isn't something you wanted, is it?' she said, appearing to be even more upset than me. I almost felt obligated to give her some kind of comforting hug.

'Not really, no.'

We both sat there in silence for a second. I tried to decide if a 25-year-old nurse could answer my question about the possibility of a single sperm having gastro, but she seemed to be really emotionally affected by my test results, so I thought it best not to add to her stress.

'Okay, so, um, thanks,' I said, and left the tiny room.

Fucknugget.

I hobbled over to the doctor's room. He reacted the same way as the nurse.

'So, what are your plans?' he asked.

'Oh, abortion. Definitely,' I quickly replied.

He nodded, and reached behind him for a pamphlet that was hidden behind a pile of other pamphlets – the pamphlets on show at the front clearly weren't meant for slutty girls who had screwed up their lives.

He handed it to me, without speaking. It was for a place called the 'Pre-Term Clinic', also known as the 'You Fucked Up So Bad The Doctor Hides This Pamphlet Behind The Other Pamphlets Clinic'.

'So … Do I just … Can I just walk in or whatever? This afternoon?' I asked.

I was clueless. As far as I was concerned, I was getting that thing taken out immediately. I didn't like that my defence system had been compromised. Also I just really wanted to stop the vomit.

'Well, you're only at about four weeks, so you may have to wait a while yet. But make an appointment to discuss it with them.'

Wait a while yet? Say what now?

'Why would I have to wait a while?' I asked, panic rising along with more vom.

'You really should speak to them about it,' he snapped back. He really, really did not want to be talking about this with me.

I took my naughty girl pamphlet and left, dialling the 'Pre-Term Clinic' number before I was even out the door.

The clinic was less than a kilometre away, across the city, in an unassuming, nondescript building. It certainly wasn't immediately obvious that it was an abortion clinic. There weren't even any protesters, which, to be honest, I was mildly disappointed about. I really wanted to see someone holding up a graphic sign while singing Bible hymns through angry tears. I wanted to walk past them in defiance. But there were just a few office workers. A café. That's about it, really. A perfectly normal city street.

The only sign that this was a 'special' kind of clinic was the prison-like locked security door. You couldn't just walk into this place. You had to push a buzzer, after which someone would look at you through a camera and ask you to identify yourself over the intercom. If you had an appointment, they'd buzz you in to a locked glass area, where the staff at reception could get a look at you and decide if you were a legitimate woman in need or a crazy person holding up a graphic sign while singing Bible hymns through angry tears. If you passed the visual test, they unlocked the final door and let you through.

In my appointment, it was confirmed that I would indeed have to wait to get this thing out of me. The lovely yet no-nonsense female doctor told me I wasn't 'far enough along' to get the termination done at that early stage. This was bizarre information to me. Not far enough along? I was supposed to let it get bigger? Allow the hostile take-over to continue?

Apparently, yes. I needed to be at least six weeks, but preferably eight, to guarantee that the 'procedure' would be successful.

I burst into tears. 'That's a month away!' I cried. 'I'm so sick and I'm throwing up more than I ever have in my life and I seriously think the sperm that broke through has gastro and I don't know how it beat the others when it's clearly defective and I can't take this for another month seriously I can't!'

'We really don't like to do it any earlier than that, I'm afraid,' she replied, politely ignoring my near-hysterical babbling.

'But what if it's a bad sperm?' I implored. 'I seriously think a bad one got through. It is not normal to be this sick. It's infecting me!'

She took a deep breath and smiled – the kind of polite smile that people give when it's taking everything within the deepest depths of their soul to be patient with the idiot in front of them.

'That's just morning sickness,' she said. 'Nausea is totally normal during a pregnancy, especially at this early stage. It's not really possible for a single sperm to … have gastro.'

She started rattling off something to do with ginger and lemonade and taking deep breaths, but I was done listening. As she continued to talk about what the termination would involve, all I could think was how stupid I had been to let this happen. My grandmother, my mother and my older sister had all been pregnant before twenty-one, and I was so cocky in my belief that I would avoid going down that road. And now, not only had I failed to break the family curse of becoming a host body before twenty-one, I was also essentially homeless. And directionless. And I couldn't afford to dye my regrowth. What a fuck-up.

After years of being sent back and forth between my alcoholic mother and a variety of different concerned adults willing to step in, I was finally removed from her care permanently at fourteen. My uncle Ben took me in, sent me to a very fancy boarding school and tried to give me some stability and consistency in what was left of my childhood. At twenty, though, that childhood was over, and he asked me to move out.

I didn't really have anywhere to go, so I just sort of floated around for a while, staying on different couches. I spent half my time on my best friend Tony's fold-out in Kings Cross, and the other half going between my older sister Rhiannon's house and my mum's house, both in Liverpool in Sydney's west. I'd stopped going to drama school because I couldn't afford the fees my uncle had been helping me with, so now I could basically be described as: Rosie, homeless cinema worker, cleaning up popcorn and busting guys getting secret hand jobs off their girlfriends during *Fast and Furious* movies.

I was hoping to work enough so that I could afford to move into a share-house close to the city, at which point I would re-assess and try to actually do something with my life. I wanted to go to university, be a writer, maybe even put that time at drama school to use. But at that stage, I was living across three different couches and pulling clothes as needed out of the boxes I had stashed in my mum's garage.

What a perfect time to get pregnant.

It was a one-night stand. A guy I met on Purple Sneakers night at a bar called The Abercrombie, in Chippendale. (Pause while every guy who went to Purple Sneakers back around 2009 tries to remember if they hooked up with me. If you were a skinny hipster and an arsehole, probably.) We made out a bit. Then he mentioned that he lived close to my sister, so we got the same train home together. Then I accidentally got off at his stop instead of my sister's and accidentally went to his house and accidentally had sex with him. I was on the pill, and we used a condom, so that defective little sperm must have been really fucking determined. I didn't have this guy's number; I didn't even know his last name. It was just a random hook-up that I didn't think would be memorable in any way.

And now I was the one sitting in an abortion clinic, being told I would have to leave this thing inside me for another month before I could do anything about it. I was also the one who had to worry about paying for it, since it was going to cost around $800.

'I'm sorry, *how much*?' I said, thudding back to reality upon hearing such an unexpected number.

'That's if you get a general anaesthetic,' the doctor replied. 'Which means you'll be put completely to sleep during the procedure. But most women just get the twilight sedation, which means you'll still be asleep, but it's not as invasive as a general. It's more like a light sleep.'

'And how much is the twilight sedation?' I asked, praying for a much lower number.

'About $400, so half as much. I really recommend that option for you. There's no reason you would need a general.'

So I had to pay $400 to be 'put to sleep but only kind of' and then, from what I could gather, have something shoved up into my uterus that acted like a vacuum. Apparently there wouldn't be pain, but 'discomfort', which everybody knows is code for 'there will definitely be pain'.

This was bullshit. If men had to get abortions, they would come in chocolate form, be less than $10 and available at every convenience store.

I booked in for a termination, performed under twilight sedation, for four weeks' time. Then I caught the train to my mum's house and spent the night puking.

Then I spent the next day puking. And the next night puking. And the next day after that. It just wouldn't stop. After a few days I realised I wouldn't be able to leave my mum's house. I could barely walk to the bathroom without being sick, let alone catch the train into the city to clean up popcorn at the movies. I lied and told them I had pneumonia and wouldn't be able to come in for a couple of weeks. Then I left the couch and went upstairs to one of mum's spare bedrooms. It had a single bed that had apparently belonged to some flatmate Mum had been sharing with for a while. Other than a bedside table, the rest of the room was empty. It was very sad and very, very grimy. The kind of room you imagine the police raiding to find evidence after a creepy man with a thin moustache gets busted masturbating on a train. And the only evidence they find is a collection of ceramic clowns.

But I was desperate, and if I was going to be staying at my mum's for a while, I needed to be in a room where I could close the door to escape her drinking. I couldn't find any sheets, so I laid a towel down on the mattress to protect me from the germs of what I was now convinced was Masturbating Train Man's bed. I covered myself with a doona riddled with cigarette burn-holes and tried to sleep.

A few days later, the nausea still hadn't relented. I spent my days trying to sleep, waking up, puking, trying to eat, puking, trying to sleep again. My older sister Rhiannon, who'd had a daughter, told me that maybe I should go to the doctor, because she did not remember being that sick during her own pregnancy. But the doctor at the clinic had told me it was normal, so I just decided to stick it out. I developed complete tunnel vision to get through it: I just had to last four weeks until it would be over. And half of the first week was already done. Rhiannon brought over a crappy little TV from her house. It only picked up Channel Nine and Channel Ten, but I switched it on and bunkered down. TV could get me through anything.

I hoped at some point the nausea would stop, but it just kept going. I was still having trouble getting up. I would go downstairs to the kitchen to mix powdered chicken stock with water, but I had to pull a chair over to the stove because I couldn't stand for the ten minutes it took the water to boil. It was like being permanently carsick, but the car could never pull over and also it was spinning. If there is a god besides Oprah, he was certainly punishing me for having sex with a guy just because he lived close to my sister's house.

Mum was working during the days and was drunk most of the nights, so I was pretty much on my own. Every couple of days when Rhiannon had time, she would bring me Gatorade and soup, but other than that, it was just me and my little TV, picking up Channel Nine and Channel Ten.

The first week passed. Then the second. Then the third. I actually felt like I was being tortured. I was desperate to get out of the house, but every time I tried to stand, nausea took over. I was starving, but every time I tried to eat, nausea took over. I was exhausted, but every time I tried to sleep, nausea took over. Nothing made it better. I'd lost weight. I was pale. I hadn't showered. I knew the Channel Nine and Ten daytime TV schedules by heart.

The day before my appointment, I'd had enough. I called the clinic, in tears, and begged them to let me bring it forward a day. I'd barely heard the word 'yes' before I was on the phone to Rhiannon, pleading with her to come and pick me up and drive me into the city.

I had to lie down in the back seat of her car for the 45-minute drive. I was so weak she had to help me walk to the clinic. At that stage, their prison-like security door was not holding me back from getting in that building – I would have smashed my way through if necessary. I was tapped into some Hulk-style determination to have this over with.

When inside, I was first taken to a side room to see the doctor. I told her what I'd been going through the last four weeks – that I basically hadn't left my bed since I'd been there last, and that it was probably a bed that a Masturbating Train Man with a ceramic clown collection had slept in, so clearly I was serious. I told her that I hadn't been able to stand up in the shower, let alone work. All I'd eaten was dry toast and soup and sips of Gatorade, and even that had been impossible to keep down. Even sitting upright in front of her at that moment was taking it out of me. 'Oh,' she said, concerned. 'That's not normal. It sounds like you have Hyperemesis Gravidarum. It can be very serious. You really should have called or seen your GP.'

This time, I was the one to give the polite smile that people give when it's taking everything within the deepest depths of their soul to be patient with the idiot in front of them. But I was too faint and too damn sick to get angry. Not to mention, last time I was there, I had rambled hysterically about an individual sperm having gastro, so I couldn't really blame her for not having taken me more seriously at the time.

Most people have only heard of Hyperemesis Gravidarum (HG) because it's the thing Kate Middleton had when she was pregnant with the first of her royal spawn. Buckingham Palace mentioned it in a brief, polite statement, which made it sound like Kate was having a bit of a hiccup but was otherwise well. I know different. If Kate was going through anything like what I went through, there is no doubt in my mind that she is probably the first person in history to have ever yelled obscenities at the Queen from the bathroom floor.

I can just see the Queen, in her sensible pastel two-piece suit, enquiring as to whether Kate would bother getting out of bed today, since ribbons that open flower shows don't just cut themselves. Kate, in a room down the hall, would wipe vomit from her face and yell, 'GO CUT A RIBBON WITH YOUR DICK, LIZ,' before burying her face back in the decorative Wedgwood toilet. I think the Queen would like Kate's spunk.

HG is officially described as 'a complication of pregnancy that is characterised by severe nausea and vomiting such that weight loss and dehydration occur. Signs and symptoms may include vomiting several times a day and feeling faint. It is more severe than morning sickness. Simple things such as taking a shower, driving or shopping may feel impossible.' (Thanks Wikipedia! Also, thanks for my Bachelor's degree.)

Unofficially, I would describe HG as 'so torturous I didn't care that I was sleeping on a mattress that was probably once owned by a Masturbating Train Man with a ceramic clown collection'. That's how badly I needed to be lying down, all day, every day.

I was sent into another room to get an ultrasound, which the technician told me was to make sure everything was in order for the 'procedure'. I thought it was strange that she didn't just say the word. Abortion. We're all here to get abortions. We're in the building; I think we know the word. She also turned the screen away from me so I wouldn't 'have to see' what was on it. I told her I didn't mind, and I honestly didn't. I wasn't in a mindset yet where I understood that this could be a painful decision for some women to make, because to me, it was nothing but a relief. Not because of the sickness I'd endured, but just because I didn't want to be pregnant. It was my body, and I didn't want this to be happening to it. I didn't feel guilty, or conflicted, or tormented. I just felt relief.

I went back out to the waiting room and sat next to Rhiannon. One woman was crying at reception. Rhiannon told me the woman and her boyfriend had been in a huge fight out the front on the street, and now she was telling the staff that she didn't think she could go through with it. She wanted to terminate, he didn't. He had stormed off and she was worried he would break up with her if she had the 'procedure'. She was worried a man would break up with her for exercising control over her own body. I was just thinking how relieved I was that I didn't have to deal with something like that, when my name was called.

Go time.

I was led into a small changing room and given a bag with a paper gown, paper slippers and paper shower cap inside. I was told to change into those, put my clothes in the bag and hang the bag on the hook. Someone would come and get me in five minutes.

Once I had changed, I sat on the bench, waiting. The bench was high, and I felt like a little girl, with my feet swinging above the ground. I was also embarrassed, because I couldn't reach back far enough to tie the gown together properly. There were two doors – the one I came in through, and one on the other side that I assumed led into the operating theatre. It was so strange, sitting there waiting, nervous and full of adrenalin, feeling small and naked and unable to stop my feet from swinging back and forth. It's funny that it's called an operating theatre, because waiting in that little room did remind me so much of waiting to go onstage; crammed into a dark space, full of nervous energy and suddenly so aware of your body, your breath, quietly waiting in the calm before the storm of the brightly lit stage.

The other door opened, and the bright lights of the theatre room hit me. There were about three or four people in there, all in gowns, all with masks over their faces. A nurse took me by the hand and led me to the bed in the middle of the room. I put my legs up in the stirrups. I was given the drugs and I fell asleep.

The next thing I remember is like remembering a dream. I was suddenly very aware of immense pain in my body. It felt like someone was inserting a blunt knitting needle in and out of my vagina. It was being inserted deep, and fast, and I wanted it to stop. I was confused, and I couldn't open my eyes. I tried to sit up, but someone held me down. A nurse held my hand. I remember her saying over and over, 'It's alright, honey. It's alright. It's nearly done. It's nearly done.'

The pain was excruciating. I hate saying that, because I don't want to scare any woman who makes the choice to abort a pregnancy. But that was my experience. I woke up, I couldn't move, and I felt like something long, thin and hard was repeatedly being shoved deep into my vagina. It was excruciating.

Then I was sitting in a recliner chair in a different room. I don't remember how I got there, but my bag of clothes was on a table next to me. There were other women lying in beds and chairs like mine – maybe about five or six in total, all looking as dazed as I'm sure I did. A nurse brought me over some crackers and a glass of juice, and I sat for a while, trying to piece together what had just happened. I looked at the clock: about forty-five minutes had passed. I could remember being in the dark little changing room. I could remember getting on to the bed and putting my feet in the stirrups. I could remember … Pain. A lot of pain. I could remember moaning and wanting it to stop. I could remember a nurse holding my hand. And then, in the middle of my confused haze, I suddenly noticed it:

It was gone. The nausea was gone. THE NAUSEA WAS GONE!

My body finally felt like my own again. I stood up, and didn't keel over with the need to vomit. I had my life back. I changed into my own clothes and went out into the waiting room to meet Rhiannon. I just wanted to get the hell out of there. And I wanted to eat. I wanted to eat a lot of food and I wanted to eat it immediately.

'Well, where do you want to go?' asked Rhiannon, clearly a little taken aback at the sudden change in me. I was one person going into that clinic, and a very different person coming out. This person could walk. And eat. This person really wanted to eat.

'Take me to Cabramatta,' I said. 'I really want to make Peking duck pancakes.'

Now, I don't remember any of what happened next, but the way Rhiannon tells it, I walked around Cabramatta shops like a mad woman, buying all the ingredients to make Peking duck. Then she took me back to Mum's house, where I proceeded to prepare the duck, talking nonstop the whole time about feeling like I had been raped by a knitting needle while unable to move, before stuffing my face with duck pancakes for ten minutes and promptly falling asleep.

I woke up the next day happier than I had been in a long time. I went back to work cleaning popcorn at the cinema, soon moved into a share-house close to the city and started studying creative writing at university. None of which I could have done if not for my 'procedure'.

Do I wish it hadn't happened at all? Of course. Do I wish RU486 had been available at the time? Definitely. Do I wish I had picked the full general anaesthetic over the bullshit 'you may feel some discomfort' twilight sedation option? Absolutely.

But I do not regret my abortion at all. AT. ALL. I have never felt sadness, or grief, or even conflicted. I was never ambivalent. I only felt relief. My life today is what it is because I was allowed to make choices about what was best for my body.

I got pregnant. I didn't want to be. I was in a position to change that. What a privileged position for a woman to be in.

And I never slept on that Masturbating Train Man's mattress again.

(PS – get the general anaesthetic.)

I've only had one abortion.
(Two. I've had two.)

I knew it as soon as I got that familiar wave of nausea.

Fuck.

I was pregnant. Again. Less than a year after the first time. And I didn't have Kate Middleton's royal vomiting disease this time. In fact, I'd been feeling so normal that I hadn't even noticed I was pregnant, and I was already twelve weeks.

Fucking shitburgers fuckity shit fuckbag.

I don't have a lot to say about this one, really. I only bring it up because almost every time I've read a personal story about abortion, it involves being emotionally scarred beyond repair, and it also only involves going through it once. It's almost like you're allowed to talk about it, but only if it was a one-off event that you will never forget and about which you will be tormented for the rest of your days. That is the price of admission for telling your story. Safe, legal and *rare*, remember? One is forgivable, but two? You're pushing it. You're taking advantage of the system feminists fought hard to protect. You're a slutty whore from whoresville making us all look bad.

Well, I am the slutty whore from whoresville making us all look bad.

Yes, I felt like an idiot at the time, but I'm not paying the 'shame' price of admission to tell this story. I've had two abortions and I wasn't emotionally scarred by either of them. It may not be the story people like to hear, but I'm still allowed to tell it. Because while I completely understand and empathise with the women who did struggle, and continue to struggle, with their choice to terminate, I know there are just as many women like me. Women who have felt nothing but relief. Women who have had more than one. Women who feel guilty that they don't feel guilty enough. Those women have stories too. And I rarely hear them. So:

I've had two abortions, and I regret neither.

(PS – the second time, I got the general anaesthetic.)

'Wait, Josephine ... I'm, um ... Wait.' My brain was trying to change reality through ... what? A stalling tactic? C'mon, Rosie. 'What happened?' I asked.

'We're not totally sure yet, details are still coming through from Austin. But Sarina talked to someone there last night.'

Oh god. His sister, Sarina. His family. His Griffith.

'It looks like he was swimming by himself, and he had a seizure and he drowned.'

'Are you sure? I mean, are you sure?'

'Apparently a nurse walked by the pool at his apartment complex and saw him floating there and pulled him out and revived him, but he died later at the hospital.'

'I ... He had told me about a seizure a few weeks ago, but he said it was ... I'm so sorry, Josephine. I'm so, so sorry.'

We talked for about another ten minutes, having a bizarrely logical conversation about details and plans, in which neither of us cried. Crying would make it real, and I still wasn't convinced that it was. Plus, there was a job to do – I needed to contact all of Tony's non-Griffith friends and tell them what had happened. His family didn't want anybody close to him finding out on social media, so I offered to make the calls. I didn't know how else I could help, but that was one thing I could do.

After I hung up, I just stood there, in my pyjamas, on my balcony, holding my phone. My brain was racing as fast as it was frozen. I looked out over the park my apartment faced. The sky was grey and it was sprinkling rain; a slight howl in the wind shook the trees. I fixated on the dark Melbourne clouds above me, trying desperately to cling to the feeling that he was still around, even though my brain now knew he wasn't. It was like trying to grab air with my fingers: I was reaching for something that I would never be able to hold. I was trying to force my mind into where it had been half an hour before, when everything was still the same. But my brain wouldn't let me. Too big of a seismic shift had occurred. And now the clouds that I was staring at were clouds that existed in a world without Tony. How could that be? And how could I only have noticed the world's emptiness now? Tony had died almost three days earlier. It had taken that long for the hospital to get in touch with people he knew in Austin, and for those people to get in touch with Tony's family in Griffith.

I had been at high tea while Tony was lying in a morgue. He was only twenty-nine.

How had my soul not shattered the second his left this earth? Tony was the longest and most significant relationship I'd ever had with a person outside my family. How had I joked about *The Sixth*

Sense with my niece and not even had an inkling that something was wrong? How had everything just ... kept going? For three days?

Shit. My niece. I opened the balcony door and stepped back into the living room. Allira looked at me nervously from the couch.

'Did you hear that?' I asked.

She nodded.

'Tony's dead. Tony's dead. He died. He had a seizure and he drowned. He's dead.' The words sounded so ridiculous coming out of my mouth. I didn't know what to do. I suppose I needed to call people. My older sister, Rhiannon, should be first. Tony, in his brilliant ability to get along with anyone, was like the brother my three sisters and I had never had. He fit so seamlessly into our little family that it was like he had grown up with us. My sisters adored him. They probably liked him more than they liked me.

I dialled Rhi's number. 'Hey, bitch,' she said jokingly, as she picked up the phone. It sounded busy on her end, like she was in a public place. She probably just figured I was calling to tell her how Allira was.

'Hey, where are you?' I asked. She was having brunch with her partner and their son, Allira's little brother Mohammed.

'What is it?' she said, her tone shifting from the silly way she had answered the phone. She could tell something wasn't right.

'Um, Tony died,' I said. It was the first time I'd ever told someone that a person had died. Whenever I watched people do it in the movies, it had always bothered me when they said someone was 'dead'. Like,

'I'm so sorry, Mrs Smith, your son is dead.' I'd always imagined that if I ever had to break this kind of news to someone, I would say 'died' instead of 'dead'. Dead was just so harsh. I mean, wow, have some empathy, movie people.

Maybe that was why I said it to Rhiannon the way I did. But honestly, I didn't even think of the words before they came out of my mouth.

She started crying instantly, before she even said anything. I was surprised at how her body immediately responded so emotionally. I was jealous that she was brave enough to open that box. I still had the lid firmly on. Crying made it real. Plus I wasn't sure that once I started, I'd be able to stop.

Rhiannon sat at a table in the middle of a crowded restaurant while I told her what happened. I asked her to call our younger sisters, Tayla and Isabella. I hung up. Next person.

Jacob. I had to call Jacob. If Tony had one part of my soul, Jacob had the other. He was another person I'd met on the first day of drama school, and, along with Tony, was one of the closest friends I'd ever had. He lived in Melbourne, but he travelled a lot for his very fancy job, so as I dialled his number, I was desperately hoping that he would be in town. He was.

Probably the most pragmatic and logical person I know, Jacob had a very different reaction to Rhiannon. He needed details, answers. It didn't make sense to him, and he initially treated it like a problem that could be solved. He asked me what felt like a million questions, but eventually he heard in my voice that I was serious, and that's when I heard his voice crack on the other end of the line.

'I'm going to leave work as soon as I can and come to your house to help you make those calls.'

'I think I'm going to get drunk,' I said.

'Yes. Smart. Numb everything. But wait for me. We can drink together. I love you. I'll be there as soon as I can.'

Next up was Mia, the only adult friend I had who would know what to do in a situation like this. I was still on my balcony in my pyjamas. I didn't know what I was supposed to do.

Neither Mia nor myself are phone-talkers. Using the phone for talking seems so archaic to me. Also I'm terrified of it. From the moment my mum started making me book my own doctor's appointments, I've had an irrational hatred of talking on the phone. I do it with close friends and family only, and even then only occasionally. My voicemail message says the following:

'Hi. You've reached Rosie Waterland. I'm thirty, which means I'm too terrified to talk to people on the phone. So, if you'd like to get in touch, please send me a message or email me! That way, I can contact you in a way that doesn't terrify me, and we don't have to talk on the phone. Okay, thanks. Bye!'

So, for me to call Mia rather than text or email her was strange. She picked up immediately, light-hearted confusion in her voice. 'Hello! Why are you calling me on the *phone*?' she asked, laughing.

'Hey, Mie.'

'What's wrong?' Just like Rhiannon, her tone changed instantly.

'Um ... Tony died.'

'What?' Like Rhiannon again, I could tell Mia was crying already. How did they just cry like that? Why wasn't I? How did they just, believe it?

I told her what happened, a story I was going to have to repeat at least thirty more times that day.

'I don't know what to do, Mia,' I finally admitted. 'I don't know what people do. I ... What am I supposed to do?'

She morphed into helpful mode. 'Okay, well, first of all, is Jacob down there?'

'Yes.'

'Make sure he comes over. You need to be around people that knew Tony and loved him like you did. You also need to send Allira home. You can't be worrying about taking care of her when you're dealing with this. I can book a flight for you if you want?'

'No, no, that's okay, I can do it.'

'Okay. Now, Rosie, you're in shock, so you need to be careful about what you do this afternoon. Don't walk near busy roads, don't go to crowded places. Try not to cook anything. Your brain and body is all adrenalin right now – it won't be working like usual.'

'Mia. You know I never cook.'

We both laughed. We laughed. This day was bizarre.

After calling a few more people, I came inside from the balcony, looked at Allira and said, 'Let's walk to the shops.' The shops were crowded, and you had to walk along a busy road to get to them. Sorry, Mia. But I just needed to be doing something. Anything. Also I needed to buy vodka, which I would definitely be drinking later. And Allira seemed to be feeling better after that stomach bug, so she would need some lunch. Shops. Walking. Lunch. Tony's dead. This day was bizarre.

Jacob arrived early that evening.

'What the fuck?' I said, as I opened the door. 'Seriously. What the fuck? What the fuck is going on?'

Allira went to my bedroom (the poor thing had no idea what to do), and Jacob and I sat, and drank, and talked about Tony. We talked about the night the three of us got drunk at his apartment in Kings Cross, then walked to the supermarket while hiding behind Jacob, who was wearing a giant cape we'd taken from the costume department at drama school. With Tony and me under the cape, it looked like Jacob had a massive arse, which, to three drunk 22-year-olds, was clearly the most hilarious thing we had ever experienced. We talked about the night the three of us went skinny-dipping in the ocean pool after watching one of our teachers in *A Midsummer Night's Dream* at Coogee Beach. I jumped on Jacob's back in the water, and he screamed as my pubes brushed up against him, while Tony watched from the sidelines, too body-conscious to fully strip down. Eventually, after Jacob and I promised to turn our backs, he pulled his clothes off and jumped into the water, spending the next ten minutes screaming as I chased him around the pool threatening to rub my pubes up against him as well.

Later that night, hair still wet, we turned up at Club 77 and danced until 6am. It was just one drunken, fun night from ten years ago, and now it seemed like a sad and profound memory. All of a sudden, the night we went skinny-dipping had so much emotional weight to it. I couldn't remember the colour of the cape at the supermarket, and it really bothered me. Silly details were now important ones. I wanted to remember everything, vividly.

We started making the calls. There was everybody from our year at drama school. The new friends he had made when he went back to drama school to study more. People he had worked with. The people he studied with in his media production degree at UTS. People I knew he had dated.

We started with those who were closest to him and worked our way down the list. Jacob and I took random turns – if he knew someone better he would make the call, and vice versa for me, although I felt obligated to make most of them.

Call after call after call after call. I came up with a sort of script in my head to follow.

'Hi, it's Rosie.'

'Oh my gosh, Rosie! Hi! It's been so long/so great to hear from you/can't believe you're calling me on an actual phone!'

'I'm actually calling with some bad news: are you able to talk now? It's about Tony. He died. There was an accident ...'

I'd answer all their questions, tell them that I was starting a Facebook group message to keep everyone up-to-date with details about the funeral, and then I'd stay on the phone with them until they felt okay to hang up. Some people cried. Most were just shocked. Speechless, almost. Everybody asked how I was, but especially how his family was. Some people wanted to get off the phone immediately. Others wanted me to stay on the line while they sat in silence or sobbed.

There were people we had to track down overseas. People who were at work. People whose partners had to get them out of the shower.

Jacob and I just sat in my living room, making call after call after call after call. I was treating it like a job. I was numb to it. It felt like I was operating a grief conveyer belt.

After making all the calls to people who had a special connection with Tony, there were still countless others who needed to be told before they saw it on Facebook or Instagram. But after making at least thirty calls that night, repeating Tony's death over and over and over and over, I couldn't do it anymore. We needed to triage grief. Most important people to Tony first, with calls. Slightly less important people next. Slightly less important people than that, a written message or email. I asked Jacob to go through my phone and message the people who might want to know, but who I didn't want to contact – ex-boyfriends and such.

Then came the calls to people who already knew. His friends in Austin, who'd not known where he was for twenty-four hours before having to identify his body and contact his family on the other side of the world. Tony's sister, Sarina. His father, Pat. His mother, Mary, was too distraught to talk on the phone. Griffith was in mourning.

When it was close to midnight, we were done. We had contacted everyone we could think of to contact. We switched off the conveyer belt of grief.

Allira went home the next day, and Jacob spent the next few nights coming to my apartment after he finished work. We mainly just got drunk and watched funny movies, sporadically stopping to have long conversations about Tony. When his family were okay with it, I shared news of Tony's death with my followers on social media. They had come to be fans of his too – he appeared in most of my photos and videos, I had written about him in my first book, and they'd all met him when they'd come to my events. He took everybody's photos during my book signings, and would always secretly flip the person's camera around and take a few selfies for them to randomly find in their photos. In the days after I revealed he had died, countless people sent me the selfies he had secretly taken on their phones. Every one of them made me laugh. It was so Tony.

I had asked my literary agent to cancel all my work commitments, so I was mainly spending my days numbing any and all possible feelings. I'd binge-watch TV all day, then get drunk at night. Some nights I was forcing myself to drink even if I didn't feel like it – it just seemed to be the easiest way to self-medicate. I was giving in to dissociative behaviour – a coping mechanism I developed during traumatic times in my childhood. I basically had the ability to leave my brain – not unlike driving somewhere and then being unable to remember anything about the trip once you've arrived at your destination. Children with abusive childhoods very often fall into periods of dissociative behaviour when their brains feel like they need to shut down for their own safety. I spent years as an adult recognising and learning to manage that behaviour, but when Tony died, I fell right back into it. The pain was just too much, and my brain recognised the feeling of trauma, so it kicked into action. I could watch four hours of television and not remember a single thing I'd seen. I'd cut myself on the bottoms of my feet, and pick at the bleeding skin for hours, not realising I'd done anything or that any time had passed, until I went to walk and felt immense pain. I would count things, anything – lines in the floorboards, spots on the carpet, patterns in tiles. Then I'd look up and see that three hours had gone by. Someone who has grown up around abuse and trauma is very skilled at stepping out of their brain.

A few days after the death, I was sitting at home in the middle of the day, watching TV in my bedroom and letting time wash over me. Eventually I realised I was hungry, so I made a bowl of Rosie's Chicken Soup and, the second it was ready, hurriedly brought it back to my room. My dark sanctuary. My blanket fort. I put the soup down on my bedside table and got into bed. I turned the TV on, then reached over to pick up the bowl. The bowl was boiling hot, and reflexively, I dropped it.

I dropped boiling hot soup all over myself. Or, more specifically, I dropped boiling hot soup all over the side of my bum. I immediately jumped out of bed and pulled my pants off, but it was too late – my skin was already starting to bubble. I ran into the bathroom and bent over comically under a cold shower, trying to get the water to hit only the burned skin and not the rest of my body on what was a freezing Melbourne winter's day.

I didn't bother cleaning up the soup. I didn't care. I just put a towel down on top of the mess and got right back into bed, awkwardly lying on the one bum cheek that wasn't burning in pain. I didn't really mind the pain though. It was distracting, and not nearly as painful as thinking about what I didn't want to think about. I fell asleep at one point, and when I woke up, the burn looked worse, not better, so I called Rhiannon.

'Rosie, it sounds like you might get an infection. You really need to go to the doctor and get it dressed properly.'

'Yeah,' I said. I had no intention of going to the doctor.

'Seriously, Rosie. If you don't look after burns they can get really bad. Have you put anything on it?'

'Well, there are too many blisters and I'm scared I'm going to pop them. Remember that time my back blistered up from that sunburn, and Grandpa popped them all when he gave me a hug? That hurt like a motherfucker. And it was gross. Stuff came out of them.'

'Go to the doctor tomorrow, Rosie.'

I didn't go to the doctor. But, by the next day, I was sufficiently worried enough about gangrene that I decided to call Jacob.

'Hey, when you come over tonight, can you bring, like, some burn stuff?'

'What do you mean "burn stuff"?'

'Well, I burned my bum with boiling hot soup, and now it's all blistered up and Rhiannon says I should put burn stuff on it. And like, a bandage or something. Plus I'm scared I'll get gangrene.'

Jacob arrived after work with a cream he'd bought and some Band-Aids, but when I pulled my pants down to show him the burn, he immediately decided we needed more.

'Nope. Nope. Nope. Nope. We're going to the doctor. Right now.'

I really did not want to leave the house. I hadn't showered or changed my clothes in days.

'No! It's fine! I just need you to put the cream on it because I can't reach.'

'Rosie. You need to dress that, properly. I didn't realise it was so ... big. We're going to need bigger bandages. And I want to ask a doctor about infection.'

It was almost 8pm, so most doctors were closed, but I agreed to go to the chemist. I didn't even change, I just put a coat on over my pyjamas. I showed the pharmacist my bum. She seemed shocked, and gave us about three different anti-bacterial creams and ointments and a bunch of bandages. Then we went home, and Jacob cleaned my bum. He rubbed anti-bacterial ointment on my bum. He rubbed soothing stuff on the blisters on my bum. Then he bandaged my bum with special burn bandages, made especially for bums.

Jacob was one of two people on the planet I would trust to clean my bum. The other person was Tony. Tony really believed in the 'universe'. He believed in energy and spirits and everything having meaning and people moving on to some kind of higher realm after they die. I really wanted to believe that too. I wanted to believe that somewhere, Tony was laughing his head off, knowing that the only time I'd felt okay in the days since he died was knowing that there was someone besides him in my life who I could rely on to clean and bandage my bum.

I will never pose naked.
(Whoops.)

At the end of 2015, I accidentally fell into a bit of a social media scandal. It all started when I put up a post on my Facebook, Instagram and Twitter at about 11pm on a Sunday night, not thinking anything would come of it.

By the next evening, the post had been seen by millions of people and was a nationally trending topic of conversation. Of course, that may have something to do with the fact that the post included a naked photo of me. A naked selfie, actually, because that's how the kidz roll these days and I try to keep up with my hip contemporaries.

The reaction was completely unexpected, although many people have told me they don't believe that (I'm honestly not that media savvy). It lasted about a week and put the time I spent as an online writer into a whole new perspective. When you become the topic other people are writing about, you really notice how pointless – and often pointlessly nasty – a lot of that opinion and critique can be.

Someone does something. Someone writes an opinion about what that person did. Someone writes an opinion about that opinion writer's opinion. Someone on the radio says something about the opinion pieces. Someone else writes an opinion about the person on the radio's opinion. The person on the radio writes a tweet, which online news sites then write entire articles about. Someone new jumps into the fray and writes an opinion about how we shouldn't be so obsessed with the story in the first place. The morning shows debate about said thing on TV. More opinion is written about the debate that just happened on TV. A new person does a new thing, the whole cycle starts again …

I can't believe I was part of that system for a few years – just churning out opinion after opinion, every day, in a news entertainment industry that relies on writers being willing and able to do that, because writing opinions about opinions about opinions helps to fill the desperate need for constant content. If you're always writing about what everybody else is saying, you'll never run out of anything to say. And if everybody else is doing the same thing, neither will they.

But I don't think there's anything wrong with making a living that way. Some people are incredibly skilled and intelligent opinion writers, who put an incredible amount of time and care into sharing something that is worth saying. There are considered opinions, though, and there are fast-food opinions. Because of tight deadlines caused by the insatiable need for news, a lot of writers are just throwing together some thoughts in an hour, based on a Twitter fight that erupted between two commentators the night before. Fast-Food Opinions. I know this because I did it. I made money churning out content without a lot of thought. It was just the nature of the job in the industry I worked in. I was happy to be paid to be a writer (I felt lucky to be, really), but after a while, my brain just became void of opinions. I was exhausted with having to write my thoughts about everything, every day, without really having the time to even figure out what my thoughts were. It all just started to feel pointless.

And then, when I myself became the subject of one of those fast-food opinion news cycles, I realised just how pointless it all really is.

I posted one photo, and it resulted in a week's worth of content, across many media outlets. And while I was bewildered and thinking, 'Really, guys? Me?' I also knew one thing to be true – if someone else had been the one to put up that photo, I would have been writing opinion about it. I would have come into a morning editorial meeting, mentioned the photo, and have had something written before lunch, complete with hashtags that were trending on Twitter. Then someone else would have written about my opinion, someone else would have written about their opinion … And it all would have gone on as usual.

But when I was the one being written about, it allowed me to be outside the fast-food opinion cycle looking in. And that's when I realised I was just so … over it.

(I know – how narcissistic to only realise the error of my ways after I was the subject of media scrutiny. Scrutiny that I had participated in countless times. But I got there in the end, at least? I'm ashamed to say that's the best I've got: I did get there in the end. It reminds me of when someone told me my first book could be illegally downloaded on The Pirate Bay. I was so excited at first, because to me, it felt like the millennial version of making the *New York Times* bestseller list. My book was so popular that people were *stealing* it? Amazing! It took a few days for the excitement to wear off, and suddenly I found myself thinking, 'That's my money, YOU DICKS.' I stopped illegally downloading that very day, but I hate myself that it took me being personally affected to realise that it was wrong. Those pirating ads just never did anything for me. You know, the ones that were at the start of DVDs – 'YOU WOULDN'T STEAL A CAR. YOU WOULDN'T STEAL A HANDBAG. SO WHY WOULD YOU PIRATE A MOVIE?' I always thought that was such a bizarre marketing idea. Putting those three things together made pirating look like *much less of a big deal*. I mean, no, I wouldn't steal a car, I'm not a criminal, but that pirating girl was just sitting at her computer; that seemed way less bad.)

So, what exactly happened when the Fast-Food Opinion machine got a hold of a story about me? Well, settle in, my friends. Here is An Autopsy Of On An Online Scandal.

It actually started much earlier in 2015, when I wrote a piece about the likelihood of me ever posing naked, which at that point was zero. Ha. I wrote about the fact that my fat body meant if I ever did decide to pose naked, people would probably call me brave, rather than sexy.

Pearl-clutching. Whenever Kim Kardashian gets naked for a photo, it inevitably leads to quite a bit of horrified pearl-clutching. Also a bit of indignant eye-rolling, a bunch of 'put it away sweetie' status updates, and a whole lot of opinion pieces about her 'provocative' and 'overly sexual' exhibitionism. When Kim Kardashian gets naked and poses for a photo, people get uncomfortable.

Do you want to know what would happen if I got naked and posed for a photo like that? There'd be no uptight women clutching at their pearls and no indignant eye-rolling. There'd certainly be no opinion pieces asking me to tone down the sexiness.

If I posed naked for a photo like Kim Kardashian, I wouldn't be admonished for being overly sexual; I'd be celebrated for being 'brave'.

Why? Because I'm fat. And if I dared to flaunt my sexuality as a fat woman, I'd be called brave. And that is such bullshit.

I don't want to be called brave. I want someone to look at a naked photo of me and clutch their fucking pearls.

I cannot tell you how patronising it is to see a woman of my size being called brave, just for putting her body on display in a sexual fashion. It's patronising because it implies that there is something so abnormal about a fat woman's body that it would take bravery to show it to anybody. Looking at a fat woman posing for a sexy photo and calling her 'brave' (usually including a solemn head nod and some kind of #sobrave hashtag) is actually code for: 'Wow. You're obviously not sexy, so trying to be sexy makes you so, so brave.'

Um, thanks?

For a long time, I was one of the people who thought it was brave for a fat woman to insist she was sexy. 'A fat girl got naked! What a legend! Good for her!' are probably all things I've said in the past. I never understood that it could be patronising rather than empowering to label a woman as some kind of trailblazer just for taking her top off.

Then I got fat. After a lifetime in a slim body, I developed myself a nifty little eating disorder and ended up gaining a lot of weight in my mid-twenties, along with a whole new perspective on life.

Gaining weight as a woman is a little paradoxical; for every kilo that you gain, you actually lose something along with it. Respect. Visibility. Dignity. Stores willing to make clothes for you that don't just include stretchy tights and T-shirts with cartoon cats on them. I could no longer walk down the street without being yelled at for having the audacity to go outside (the very creative, 'FAT!' was something I heard almost daily). I couldn't eat in public without being sniggered at. Bouncers practically laughed in my face when I tried to get into bars with my friends. I felt like a ghost in the spotlight, invisible while being the centre of humiliating attention. But, despite having basically lost the ability to go outside and live a normal life, that wasn't the most obvious thing I lost. When I got fat, the most obvious thing I lost was my sexuality. When I gained weight, my sexuality disappeared.

It happened without me even realising it. You see, as a fat woman, society no longer puts you in the 'sexually desirable pile'. You are not playing by the rules, not providing the world with the aesthetic they expect and value in women, so you are no longer considered sexy. But not being considered sexually desirable by other people doesn't mean you don't still have sexual desires yourself. And that's where I got confused. How could I not be a sexual being if I still had sexual urges? I still felt sexy. Still masturbated. Still wanted sex. But the overwhelming sense I got from the world around me was that I was no longer invited to the club.

And it wasn't just that men didn't want to date me. Stores didn't want to dress me. Lingerie companies decided that I didn't exist once I exceeded Size 16, like it was just assumed that a woman any bigger than that would never need sexy underwear. I couldn't find myself in magazines, unless it was in a self-celebratory 'Look! We've got a fat girl this month because #diversity!' If I ever saw myself on screen, it was as the woman whose personality was great enough that a guy would be willing to 'forgive' her size. In porn, I was just a fetish, the 'BBW' (Big Beautiful Woman) who would put up with all kinds of degrading treatment because she was so desperate for any kind of sexual contact.

It was as if everybody on earth had collectively decided that I no longer had the right to be sexual. My vagina was closed for business. My body was not to be put on show. I should never look in the mirror and smile, I should just put on that cat T-shirt, forget about sex and apologise for not meeting the aesthetic standards expected of me. At twenty-six, my time as a sexy woman was done. That I still felt sexual was irrelevant. Too bad, too sad, fattie.

And that was when I realised I hated the word 'brave', because calling a woman brave for 'daring' to be sexual is just another condescending way of telling her that she isn't.

Fat women are sexual, because they are women and women are sexual. Their sexuality doesn't disappear because they don't have bodies that are considered desirable by modern, conventional standards. Sexuality doesn't work that way. Its existence can only be dictated by the person who has it. So when a fat woman considers herself a sexual being, decides to put that sexuality on display and is then called 'brave', it exasperates me. How can people not realise it's just another way of telling a woman that she's not actually sexy?

As frustrating as the 'brave' label is though, I understand that it comes with the best of intentions. Being a fat woman in today's society is not easy, and when I gained weight, I noticed that people often wanted me to know that they empathised with that fact. They wanted me to know that they understood how hard it must be for me. It's like I was considered brave just for existing in the universe as a fat woman. I was often told I was brave for working in a job that required me to be in the public eye. Seriously – just working in a job, as a fat woman, was considered brave. No wonder sexuality for fat women with the absence of bravery is a mind-boggling concept for many.

And yeah, facing discrimination for being a fat woman isn't easy. In fact, it can be fucking horrendous. But calling fat women 'brave' for putting up with that shit is not helpful. All the 'brave' label does is imply that fat women are achieving something in spite of who they are. And the 'in spite of' implies that who they are is wrong.

Insisting on existing in the universe and living life shouldn't be considered brave. Insisting on working the job you want, wearing the clothes you want and being as sexual as you want shouldn't be considered brave. It should be considered completely unremarkable. It should be considered as boring as when anyone else does it.

So please, please, if I ever decide to pose half naked in a Kardashian-style Instagram photo, messy hair falling to my nipples, bum glistening, each of its cheeks barely hiding the lacy string of my tacky G-banger, I don't want you to say that I'm 'brave'. I want you to clutch your pearls, head to your computer and write a furious op-ed about how inappropriate the whole thing is, because a naked photo of me would just be TOO DAMN SEXY.

Not fucking brave.

I filed that piece away in the back of my mind, not really thinking I would ever get the chance to find out what people would say if I posted a naked photo, because there was no way in hell I was ever going to post a naked photo.

Then I posted a naked photo. And everyone called me brave. Damn.

I'm not sure why I did it, to be honest. It was a very spur of the moment thing. I was up late one night, thinking a lot about body image, and getting sick of flawless Hollywood women complaining about their 'fat' bodies, so I took a photo of my body and posted it, along with the following text:

Alright. I can't believe I did this but …

I've been reading/watching a lot lately about women in the public eye who are implicitly arguing that they're 'brave' for being a few kilos heavier than the average fashion model. Like, not being thin automatically makes them flawed, and therefore 'brave' for daring to live their lives in the public eye. What frustrates me about these women is not that they're way thinner than me (and thus sort of implying that if they think they're some kind of fat yet successful miracle, then I must be a sea monster with no hope), but that despite their success, they still see weight as a major contributing factor to their value.

How sad. How sad, that after becoming admired trailblazers for women, they still feel the need to talk about their size, as if mentioning it is their responsibility to cancel out some kind of elephant in the room.

It shouldn't even be an issue. When you are spectacularly intelligent and talented, your appearance and weight should not even be an issue. I know as a woman, it's not easy to say that. As a woman, even if your appearance isn't an issue to you, it is to everyone else. I get that. But, fuck everyone else. We need women in the entertainment industry willing to put their intelligence and talent ahead of their looks. It may not be easy, but if we want values to change, it's necessary.

And how do we change those values? By being un-fucking-apologetic. By refusing to explain. If you find that you're successful and a woman and not 'conventionally' attractive, don't give it a second freaking thought.

Your body is your history. It's your battleground. It's what makes you who you are, and you wouldn't be as intelligent or as successful or as funny as you are without it.

I survived a childhood filled with abandonment and trauma. Then I survived mental-health struggles and eating disorders. I had weight-loss surgery and continue to question that decision. And in the end of all of that, this is me. This is my body. I have stretch marks. I have flabby skin. I have a belly. I have saggy boobs and I'm covered in freckles that made me cry when I was younger.

But I'm also a bestselling author. A famous writer. An admired and funny woman. I'm touring a live one-woman show this year. I'm attending writing festivals with my heroes. I'm writing and starring in my own TV show.

I don't look the way I'm 'supposed' to look, according to a select group of people. But I just don't give a fuck. Because I've achieved more than I've ever dreamed of in spite of people assuming I wasn't pretty or thin enough. I don't even think about being pretty or thin enough – I just think about writing the best, funniest shit I can write. My body has nothing to do with that.

So here it is. The body that was meant to hold me back. The body that I'm supposed to apologise for. The body that is meant to keep me off your screens and out of your minds. But my intelligence and my talent is more important than my appearance. And those qualities are what will force me onto your screens and into your minds. So there.

Sharing a picture like this should end my entertainment industry career. Fuck that. I can write for and play multi-faceted, complex and brilliant women because I am one. And I am one because of the life I've lived and the body that I've lived it in.

I am not flawed. I am brilliant. I am a survivor. And I make no apologies.

(And yes – I used a very flattering filter on my face in this photo. I'm posing nude, give me a freaking break.)

I put that post up, called Tony, who was in the US, to laugh about it, then went to bed. The next day, I noticed that the Fast-Food Opinion machine had started with a bang overnight. I was asked to go on TV and radio to explain myself. Countless articles and social media statuses, tweets and comments were throwing their two cents in. I freaked out, and felt like I needed to explain myself more clearly, so I put up another Facebook post.

Why write about how important it is not to focus on physical appearance, and then attach a naked photo of yourself?

Good question hahahaha.

So … This whole nudie pic thing became a much bigger deal than what I anticipated! Your reaction has been overwhelming. I will say this though:

I get that it may seem counterintuitive to post a status about how appearance shouldn't matter, and then attach a naked photo of myself. I get that. I thought a lot about that before I posted it actually. I mean, if the physical really doesn't matter and I don't want it to be an issue, why did I put up a photo that very clearly made it an issue? Well, I had a message to get across I guess, and being a bigger woman, I felt like I was in a somewhat unique position to do so visually.

I have been seeing so many women, much thinner than me, constantly talking about how they've achieved things in life in spite of their flaws. The thing that bothers me about that discourse is that 'flaws' are even being talked about at all, and so damn often. Why is the physical always so important? So high on the agenda? There just seems to be this overarching attitude that the physical should always be top on the list of values and priorities and attention.

That's why I posted the status and photo.

I highlighted my flaws to show how frustrated I am that we even obsess about flaws to begin with! A little counterintuitive, yes, but I just wanted to say, 'Look. I'm not a thin woman. In fact, I have a body that a lot of women would consider their worst nightmare. I know there are things about me that are not conventionally attractive, but I'm happy with myself because my appearance isn't what I value most about myself. So take a look at me. Take a look at this photo. Take a look at my "flawed", chubby body, and know that if I can get on with life not constantly obsessing over my looks, then you can too.'

That's why I refused all media requests today.

Because I really do believe that we should not be obsessing over appearance, so I didn't want to feed that obsession by talking more about it. I just wanted to put the post up, vent my frustration and sadness at physical appearance being such an issue for so many women, and then go back to not letting physical appearance be an issue for me. I didn't want to go on a bunch of chat shows to talk about it, because the whole point of my post is that I think people need to stop talking so much about it. There is so much more to each of us than our looks. I have reached a place in my life where understanding that has made me a lot happier as a person, and I would love to see other women reach that place too. I thought and hoped maybe a photo of me could help some women get there. I'm willing to let my appearance be a talking point for a couple of days, as long as the talking point is, 'Actually, yeah – why are we so freaking obsessed with appearance anyway?'

I'll leave the photo up as long as Facebook allows it, because I stand by the message and the way I chose to deliver it. But I don't have anything else to say about my body, because my body is THE LEAST INTERESTING THING ABOUT ME! Soon, the status will be so far down my Newsfeed that it will be forgotten, and my naked body will no longer be a talking point.

Now, I'm going to go and watch some TV and hang out with my cat. xoxoxo

Not long after that status went up, Facebook deleted the photo and blocked my account for forty-eight hours. Instagram deleted the photo and threatened to deactivate my account if I ever did it again. Twitter deleted the photo, plus they put new restrictions on my account, so whenever I post a photo on Twitter now, it's blurred with a warning telling people it may contain 'offensive content'. So I'm pretty sure Twitter thinks I'm a sex criminal.

I stepped away from the whole thing and retreated into myself. I honestly had not expected to cause such a fuss with what I considered a pretty specific feminist message about body image that would only be relevant or interesting to a few people.

The Fast-Food Opinion machine had come after me, and it really made me doubt myself. I felt like shit, basically.

I stayed true to my promise not to talk to any media about it. I don't know what I would have said if I had, because I really had no idea what I thought about anything anymore. I needed time to gather my thoughts, to spend more than an hour figuring out my opinion for a change.

I ended up taking a couple of months. I had been asked to give a talk at the All About Women Festival at the Sydney Opera House, and I decided to use that time onstage to describe exactly what had happened to me in the days and weeks after putting up a naked photo. I'd had the time to think about how the whole situation had shaped me as a woman and forced me to look at my identity, even if I didn't always like what I saw. Here's what I said that day:

> *I have been panicking, for months, that this talk is going to reveal to everyone that I'm a complete fraud. I mean, when they came to me and asked if I wanted to give a talk at the Opera House for All About Women, I was like, 'Are you kidding? Absolutely. Let me just call anyone in my life who's ever wronged me and shove it in their faces.' And just as I was in the middle of that revenge fantasy, they told me that the topic they'd assigned me was 'How to be yourself' and I instantly felt sick. Because I realised 'Oh, they think I know!' And when I get up to give a bunch of paying audience members a definitive guide on 'how to be themselves', everyone is going to realise that I have no fucking idea.*

Now, this is a problem for me, since just a few months ago I published a memoir called The Anti-Cool Girl, *which basically outlines my journey to self-acceptance and yes – figuring out how to be myself. I wrote about being born to addicted and mentally ill parents who forced my sisters and me into a childhood filled with neglect and abuse and trauma. I wrote about how that affected my sense of self and belonging and how I became convinced that if I just managed to sneak my way into the cool crowd, I'd finally feel love and acceptance. And the final chapter of my book explored my mid-twenties awakening, in which I realised that I was enough, and I just needed to care less and do what felt right for me, fist pump nailing it, etc etc etc! Follow my example and be an anti-cool girl! Be yourself! Huzzah!*

And now, I'm terrified to have to stand here and admit to you that sometimes I read that chapter and think it's full of crap.

The thing is, I do know that to be yourself, you have to know who you are. But I change my mind about who I am on a daily basis. I mean, some days, I read the chapter of self-discovery in my book, and I think: 'God, Rosie, you are so fricking wise, man, well done on having your shit together and never compromising who you are.' Other days, I read that chapter, and I think: 'God, Rosie, you suck, you don't even follow your own advice. You say it's liberating to stop caring what people think? You care what everybody thinks. You cried when you were reading your Twitter notifications yesterday. You're such a fraud.'

And now, standing here talking to you, I'm terrified you're all going to realise I'm a fraud now too, because, if you came here, based on my book, or even the topic of this talk, expecting a magic formula on how to be yourself, I have to tell you right now that I'm not going to be able to give that to you.

But, if I am going to admit that I have no idea what I'm doing and possibly ruin my career in the process, I might as well do it at the Opera House, in a flower crown and a tutu, I mean, what a way to go, am I right?

Here's what I do know: Having a clear sense of self and sticking to it is easy, in theory. But maintaining that sense of self in the face of, well, life, and reality, can often feel almost impossible. I mean, it's one thing to try and follow the philosophies of 'leaning in' or 'not giving a fuck' or 'being an anti-cool girl', but what about the days where you just can't? The days where 'leaning in' feels exhausting, and the days where you actually do kind of give a fuck and the days where rather than being an unaffected anti-cool girl, you sort of want the cool kids to like you.

I have days like that all the time, days where I just can't live up to the person I'm supposed to be, to the person that I wish I was, and it often makes me feel like a failure.

Let me give you an example of a time recently where I got completely confused about who I was, and basically had an existential identity crisis/brain fart.

So, a couple of months ago, I put a naked photo of myself on the internet. I actually haven't spoken about it since, so saying that just now makes me think 'you crazy bitch'.

Which is actually what a lot of other people thought about it too. My mum asked me if I was drunk, since the Facebook post went up quite late, and that offended me, because I hadn't just put up the photo, I had written what I considered a really articulate and well-thought-out piece explaining why I was doing it. And I said that to my mum, I said: 'Mum, I wasn't drunk! How could I be drunk and write like that, didn't you read what I wrote?' And she was like, 'Oh, no, I just saw the photo and thought you must've been pissed.' Thanks, Mum.

She wasn't the only one. A LOT of people wanted me to know what they thought about that photo. And when I say people, I mean women. There were a few men who told me to put my saggy tits away, but mostly it was women who felt like they needed to tell me why what I had done was brilliant, or why what I had done was an eye-roll-inducing embarrassment.

I was shocked at the level of reaction, which a lot of people considered a disingenuous response from me. I do have a large online following, sure, but I honestly thought when I put up the post that it was kind of a boring rant about feminism and

body image, and maybe a few hundred people on my page
would like it, and Facebook would probably take the photo
down anyway because apparently women's nipples are more
offensive than hate groups, so I just put it up and went to bed.

Cut to the next day, and my naked body was a nationally
trending topic of conversation. And the honest truth is: I was
fucking mortified. I was approached by a lot of media asking
me to explain myself, and I sort of crafted this dignified
response where I said I wasn't going to fuel the story, because
my body isn't the most interesting thing about me — and
that was partly true, but what was also true was that I was
just really freaking mortified that my naked body ended up
everywhere, and no, I didn't want to go on your TV show
and be interviewed while my boobs are displayed on a ten-foot
screen behind me. Are you kidding? This is so embarrassing!

But I am the first to admit that I had actively, yet naïvely
and inadvertently, put myself in that position. And the
vulnerability I was feeling that day was of my own making.

But, the vulnerability wasn't just about my body, it was
also about my thought process — it was about the fact that
I had made a pretty definitive statement about who I was
and something that I stood for, and then I started to question
it. Despite having put what I insisted to my mum was an
incredibly moving and articulate critique on our culture's
obsession with female appearance, a strange thing started

happening where it didn't matter what I had written, because women kept explaining to other women why I had done it. And I started reading all these women arguing about whether I was brave, or an insufferable idiot, and it was like: 'Rosie meant to say this.' 'NO she didn't, she's a fool, she means this.' And then I was just like: 'Arrrghhhh I don't even know what I meant anymore, I'm confused!'

Now initially, I posted the photo for the following reason: I'm a big girl. And my body has been through a lot. I was always quite thin, and then for a bunch of reasons I gained a lot of weight in my early to mid-twenties, and then I lost a lot of that weight, so my body has ended up in this kind of 'looks like I've had a baby but I haven't' mode. Like, I've got really stretchy skin, and I'm covered in stretch marks and I have a belly that will always be there and I can basically pinch some skin on my boobs and pull it up to my chin. I say basically like I haven't tried it but I've tried it, I know I can do it. I'd show you now but we're in the Opera House, so let's keep it classy.

So, you know, my body is, by conventional standards for a woman, considered seriously flawed. I am told by society a million different ways every day that I'm disgusting. And I've got to be honest with you, that paralysed me for a while. I, like a lot of women, had spent my life hinging my self-worth on my appearance without even realising it. But the incredibly dangerous thing about hinging your self-esteem on your appearance is you might as well be hinging your self-esteem on a house of cards. Because no matter what you inject into your face, no matter how obsessively you work out or how restrictive you are with what you put in your mouth, your appearance will change. You will age. Your face is ageing right now. Your body is ageing right now. Gravity is taking its toll right now. And if you have invested all of your self-worth on the house of cards that is your aesthetic appeal, that house of cards is eventually going to topple and you are going to feel worthless.

Now, gaining weight in my early twenties is when my house of cards came crashing down. When I gained weight, I felt like a worthless piece of shit. But that led to something incredible happening. I no longer had my appearance to fall back on to feel value, so I had to look for other things that I valued about myself. And building a new scaffolding of self-esteem not based around looks was incredibly liberating for me. I started to place more value on my intelligence. On my talent as a writer. On my ability to be a fierce and loyal friend. On my sense of humour. On the love I have for my sisters. On the fact that I survived a pretty horrific childhood filled with trauma, abuse and neglect.

And when I started valuing those things, I suddenly remembered that I had a right to be in the universe. In spite of my body, I had a right to not only exist, but to be successful and to kick arse. And I would never have realised that if I was still convinced my body and appearance were the most important things about me. Does that mean I don't care about looks at all? Of course not. I get eyelash extensions every three weeks, for Christ's sake. I love dressing up, I love make-up, I truly believe in the transformative power of fashion. But all those aesthetic-based values have just been pushed lower down my values list, because I spent a long time living with them at the top of my list, and I just ended up feeling worthless.

And so, having lived all of that, I started to get really sad that women, far thinner than me, far more conventionally attractive than me, seemed so hung up on their bodies. Eighteen-year-olds are getting lip fillers and Botox and breast implants, wellness warriors are posting photos on Instagram where they pinch a tiny roll of skin on their stomachs and hashtag it 'working on my imperfections'. (Get back to me when your stomach's so big you can't see your vagina, then talk to me about what society considers imperfect.) My thirteen-year-old-niece looks up to Kendall Jenner, a girl who openly admits all she ever dreamed for herself was to be a Victoria's Secret model. Cindy Crawford, one of the most physically genetically blessed people on the planet, announced that she was retiring from being professionally photographed at fifty, and was 'passing the torch' to her fourteen-year-old daughter.

So, I posted a naked photo of myself. Just to say: you know what, I have a body that society tells me is disgusting – here's a photo, just to prove it. Society tells me that as a woman, this body should make me feel worthless. But I don't – not because I unequivocally love my body, because I don't – I have struggles with my body image like everyone else – but because I value other things about myself, and I really encourage you to try it, because it's been so liberating for me.

That's what I meant to say.

That, however, was not what a lot of people took from the post. And that's when I started to have a 24-hour-long brain fart.

So, first of all, a lot of women were complimenting me for being 'so brave'. I understand the intention behind that, but nobody says Miranda Kerr is brave for posting a naked photo. Calling me brave was basically saying, 'Your body is not attractive, so it is really brave that you're putting it all out there.' And I was just like, 'Ah, thanks. I would have really preferred if you had told me to put it away for being too sexy, but okay.'

Then a lot of women were congratulating me on being a bigger woman who was proud of her body, and who was not afraid to flaunt it. And that also wasn't right, because I have incredibly ambivalent feelings about my body, and I wasn't comfortable being labelled as a body-image crusader. Some days I feel sexy, other days I cry about the size of my fupa. But, the point is, that on the days where I cry, I don't feel worthless because I've learned to value other things, right? Is that what I meant?

Then other women were angry that I'd shown my body at all. 'A post about how our bodies shouldn't be important is ruined by including a photo of your body,' a lot of them said. And then I sort of thought: 'Oh, it made sense at the time. I dunno, does it? Maybe you're right.'

Some women were angry that I'd said looks don't matter yet I was wearing make-up in the photo and we can tell there's a filter on it, you idiot. Well, first of all, I wasn't wearing make-up, it was just the eyelash extensions, so that critique just made me feel pretty. And as for the filter thing — of course I put a freaking filter on! I was posting a naked photo, give me a break, sheesh. And I didn't say looks don't matter, I just said they're not the most important thing. Didn't I? I DON'T EVEN KNOW ANYMORE.

Then there were just a lot of women online eye-rolling at me. The worst was a tweet from a female comedian I really like, who, and I'm paraphrasing here, tweeted something like, 'I'm finally feeling brave enough to reveal this private part of myself,' and below it was an X-ray picture of a uterus. And I was like, 'Arrrghhh that really hurts my feelings but damn it, that's a funny joke. What a solid burn.'

So, at the end of that very bizarre twenty-four hours in which my naked body had gone viral because of a photo

I'd posted myself, I was so confused about why I had done it. The Daily Mail even wrote an article about me having posted the photo because I was inspired by some blogger I've never heard of, and then I started to think, 'Oh god, maybe I have heard of her, I DON'T KNOW WHAT'S GOING ON, WAAAHHH.' And then I tried to write a follow-up explaining what I had meant to explain the first time but by that point my brain was just checking out. I mean, the women who loved it, loved it for a million different reasons, and the women who hated it, hated it for a million different reasons.

And as I was taking all of those opinions on board it was overwhelming what had been such a clear message in my mind initially. What didn't help was that, apparently, even though people were reporting the naked photo to Facebook, it wasn't taken down for more than a day. Facebook said it was because of a glitch in the system but I like to think there was some feminist staffer that day who was just like, 'Oh, I'm trying to delete it. I don't know why it's not working.'

But the photo was up long enough that the comment thread kind of reached this critical mass.

And I was feeling incredibly vulnerable, not just because a naked photo of me had reached over six million people, but because I was so overwhelmed by the response to it that I wasn't even confident about why I had put the photo up in the first place. And that's when I started to feel like a fraud.

You know, I'm meant to be 'The Anti-Cool', I'm meant to know who I am and to never question it because I don't care what people think, and after putting up that photo, I was questioning everything.

I mean, I spent a long time with a body-image specialist figuring out all that stuff I just told you and feeling really solid about it, and then all it took was a bunch of comments to make my brain explode into an identity crisis. I was just like, 'Why the hell am I going on about fragile card houses and self-worth? Stephanie Williams from Brisbane is right – YOU KNOW NOTHING, YOU INSUFFERABLE FOOL. And if you really meant it you would have taken the photo from a less flattering angle.'

Having a clear sense of self is easy in theory, but maintaining it when things get tough is hard. And I fail at it ALL THE TIME. Even in important moments when I shouldn't – like when I decide to make a statement by putting a naked photo of myself on the internet. Or when I agree to do a talk on how to be yourself, forgetting that I don't really know how.

So, what do we do? If I'm meant to be the expert and I'm standing here telling you I'm a massive fraud and I don't have a clue, then what do we do?

How do we figure out who we are, and spend every day being ourselves, when life gives us so many conflicting rules to follow, particularly as women?

Waxing your pubes is relenting to the patriarchy.

versus

Waxing your pubes is a powerful example of the autonomy you have over your body.

Don't read women's magazines or you'll be betraying the sisterhood. '24 steaming hot ways to keep him happy in bed' is an embarrassment to us all.

versus

Women's magazines provide a much needed and important platform for women. '24 steaming hot ways to keep him happy in bed' allows women to talk openly about sex.

Don't eat sugar or carbs. Take pride in your health. Sugar is DEATH and carbs are the devil.

versus

Eat whatever you want, because crazy diets are just a multi-billion dollar industry designed to keep women in a food prison.

Don't put off having kids in case your junk goes bad and your eggs die. You aren't a real woman unless you have kids. Every period is a wasted opportunity.

versus

Concentrate on your career instead of kids because that's what a man would do. Every period just gets rid of another egg that would have ruined your life.

You're only sexualising yourself because the patriarchy has forced you to.

   <u>versus</u>

   Celebrating your sexuality however you want is brave and empowering.

'Bitch' is an offensive word to women. Don't use it.

   <u>versus</u>

   'Bitch' is an empowering word for women. Use it.

Free the nipple.

   <u>versus</u>

   Don't free the nipple. That's just admitting that your body is the most important thing about you. Don't be such a slave to men's visual expectations.

If we're going to call ourselves feminists, women need to support other women.

   <u>versus</u>

   Men aren't expected to support each other all the time. Women should be able to criticise each other without it being about feminism.

*Don't say 'vagina'. Say 'vulva'. Not understanding the correct
terminology for your body is embarrassing to your gender.*

versus

   *It's your genitalia. Call that special place 'beef curtains'
or 'lady garden' or 'fish taco' or 'fanny' or whatever the hell
you want. Just make sure you say it all the time, because real
women talk about their vaginas.*

*Oh, and speaking of 'real women', be a real woman. Just
don't be too fat, too skinny, too sexy, too prudish, too
aggressive, too passive. Be a role model for all other women
but be modest enough to never think you're a role model. Have
it all, but also admit that it's impossible to have it all. Don't
screw any of this up.*

   *Seriously. Where the fuck does that leave us? In the face
of all of that conflicting noise, how are we supposed to figure
out, not only who we are, but how to remain true to that at all
times?*

   *I don't know. The best I can offer you is this: have an
idea of who you'd like to be, and aim for that, but always
embrace failure. Which I'm helpfully providing you with an
example of right now, failing at giving you the advice you came
here for.*

   *I know who I want to be, and sometimes I'm great
at it. Other times, I'm not even close. I want to not care*

*what other people think. I want to not be heartbroken that
I haven't found lasting love yet. I want to be confident in
my opinions and never waver. I want to not be sad that
Sportsgirl doesn't make clothes that fit me. I want to give
zero fucks that the cool kids think I'm lame because I don't
know any of the bands on Triple J. I want to not care that I
was meant to be on the cover of <u>Spectrum</u> this weekend and I
got bumped for the almost perfect woman that is supermodel/
PhD candidate that is Tara Moss. I want to eternally
embrace that I'm scruffy and shy and like drinking vodka
on my couch in my underpants, but I even question that
sometimes too.*

*I want to always be the Anti-Cool Girl that people think
I am, but I don't always get there.*

*We're often told that having a strong sense of self will
keep us on solid ground when life gets difficult. But I think
that accepting that your sense of self is bound to falter when life
gets difficult is the real advice we need to learn. Because it will
happen, and we need to not be drowned by feelings of failure
every time it does.*

*So, embrace the failure. Know who you want to be, but
also be okay with not knowing how to do it all the damn time.
Nobody is going to be perfect at being themselves – not even
the people who have written books about it and are asked to
give fancy talks at the Opera House.*

Let's all embrace failure. Let's all accept that we can only be perfect at being imperfect. That's about as close to being ourselves as we're ever going to get.

So that's it. That was my final opinion on the online scandal that saw me get sucked into the Fast-Food Opinion machine. A machine that I had spent a long time being a part of. I don't begrudge that machine now though, I really don't. I spend a lot of time hate-reading the *Daily Mail* Sidebar of Shame, and I will admit to still looking up Fast-Food Opinions about the scandal of the day. So I know people want to read that stuff, because sometimes I do. And I don't begrudge the people writing it, because I know that paid writing jobs are hard to come by. Somebody has to write that stuff. It's just that, after a couple of years, I was done writing it.

Posting a naked photo was the thing that made me realise that.

I still can't believe people called me 'brave', though. THAT PHOTO WAS SEXY, DAMN IT. Clutch your goddamn pearls.

Hey mon frère with your derrière, something something cush.

Something something something yeah.

It's Jack's Subway Tush.

I had been in the hospital for almost twenty hours now, and I still couldn't remember the words to that song from *Will & Grace*. I could see the exact scene in my head. It's the end of the episode, Jack is sad that his Subway Tush thing didn't work out, and he and Will are sitting in Will's living room, when they start singing the jingle. I could see them singing it. I just couldn't remember the damn words.

Hey mon frère –

Jacob had left a note for me, telling me that Jamila would be back in the morning, and he would be back at lunch tomorrow. He thought I'd been asleep when he wrote it, and hadn't wanted to wake me, but there was no way I could sleep. I just really didn't want him to feel bad about leaving. I could handle being next to the poo curtain on my own for a few hours.

Something something it's Jaaaaaaaack's Suuuuuubwaaaaaaay Tuuuuuush.

The hospital had most of the lights turned off now, which was the only way I knew it was night time. The day before, my friend Mia had flown down from Sydney to see me, and I didn't believe her when she told me it was 2pm. I was so disoriented. Since being admitted, time had both sped up and slowed down. It could have been a week or a few hours since the ambulance brought me in. I had no idea.

I did everything I could to help my sisters.
(I didn't.)

I'm the reason my little sisters got taken away. I knew that Mum was drunk, and I knew that I should stay home and take care of them. But I was selfish, and I didn't want to deal with Mum's abuse anymore, so I left.

The police had taken them by the time I got back.

We lived in a very run-down little house in the Blue Mountains, on a street that was mostly bush. There was one house next to us, one across the street, and nothing else for a few hundred metres either side. It was the kind of place that would feature in a horror movie after the car takes a wrong turn and breaks down. This street definitely wasn't from the 'we're still happy and nothing could ever possibly go wrong' part of the movie. It was more from the 'is it worth knocking on the door of that house for help when it's fairly likely that the people who live inside collect the fingers of tourists' part of the movie. It was an eerie, creepy, isolated street. But with a beautiful view!

The house belonged to Mum's latest boyfriend, who she'd met while Rhiannon, Tayla and I were living in foster care. Brian, like all of Mum's boyfriends before him, was convinced that he would be the one to save her; the one to stop her from drinking. Like he had some magic formula for sobriety that none of us had thought of yet. Even at ten years old, I would look at those guys and think, 'Oh! You mean we just have to tell her that we don't want her to drink anymore? That we didn't really enjoy having our foster dad stick his hands down our pants and we would very much like to have a mother who doesn't put us in that position again? That she just needs to be strong and choose Diet Coke instead? WHY DIDN'T WE FUCKING THINK OF THAT?'

When we first arrived at Brian's house, there was a giant Confederate flag hanging on the main wall in the living room. 'Oh good,' I thought. 'Mum's choice in men continues to be top notch.' (Seriously – if you were dating someone, got back to their place for the first time and saw that on the wall, how could you not immediately push life's panic button and get the hell out of there?) But besides smoking pot twenty-four hours a day (which essentially turned the house into a giant Dutch oven – I'm sure I was permanently stoned from ages nine to fourteen), I thought he was a nice guy at the time. I didn't know any better.

Just another guy who got caught in my mother's irresistible web, and planned to revolutionise the way alcoholism was treated – maybe even cure it! – through the power of love.

He did not cure alcoholism through the power of love. If he had, I would have been pissed off, to be honest, since Mum's love for her daughters hadn't cured anything. She would always love booze most of all (wine in a box was her favourite), and if she wouldn't give it up for us, at least she wasn't giving it up for someone else. That would have stung.

Brian did what he could though. He was the one who picked me up when I faked a broken ankle to get out of running cross-country. Granted, I faked the broken ankle because he had initially refused to pick me up and I wasn't entirely sure how I was going to get home, so I figured an ambulance could get the job done. (I hadn't anticipated the ambulance would take me to the hospital and not just conveniently drop me off at my front door after maybe stopping at Maccas on the way.)

It all started when I came third in my primary school cross-country. I can't remember how long it was, I think only about three kilometres, but I was not even close to being an athletic person. Sports, and the obligation to compete in organised sporting activities, was abhorrent to me. As far as my PE teachers were concerned, I had permanently had my period from birth, and would therefore be unable to climb that rope/swing or bat/torture myself in your horrific 'beep test'.

When I ended up in a private school in Year 10, where sport is considered more important than learning to read, my period excuse was often dismissed by the female teachers, who seemed to have this magical way of knowing that I could not possibly have blood gushing out of me twenty-nine days of every month. Aware that I needed to try a different tack, I started earnestly telling them that I couldn't participate in PE because I had 'a bone in my foot'. I would always say it quietly, like I found it humiliating; like I was sharing a shameful secret with them that only a select few knew. At first I just wanted to see if I could use a ridiculously idiotic excuse to successfully get out of physical activity. I never dreamed that anyone would take it seriously.

'So, you have a ... *bone*. In your foot?'

'Yes,' I would reply, looking sad, with my head down. 'I do.' Yet, while I was quietly thinking, 'Who fucking doesn't, you idiot?' it appeared, in my efforts to be a smartarse, I had lucked onto a bizarre excuse that actually worked.

'Oh, okay,' the teacher in charge would reply, looking concerned. 'You should probably sit this one out.'

I never had to do the beep test again.

But back in Year 6, at a tiny Blue Mountains public school, there was no getting out of cross-country. It was a class activity that everyone had to participate in, no matter how many periods I insisted I ... had. (I didn't exactly understand how periods worked at that stage.)

I suppose, given I was ten and sprightly and TV still only had five channels, I was accidentally fit. Because about two minutes into the three-kilometre race, I found myself coming first. It was a complete shock to me – I had not expected to make it once around the oval, and here I was, one lap in, in the lead, and not even tired. I started to fancy myself as some kind of superhuman. Clearly, I had an untapped skillset that could only be explained by my having been born an exceptionally gifted athlete, which I was only now just discovering. I would need to change my whole life plan. Writing for television was out. I needed to pivot my fantasies of winning an Emmy and an Oscar to winning Olympic Gold. I was built to have the wind flowing through my hair, I was meant to be a runner, I was meant to wear an ugly green and gold suit during the opening ceremony, I was meant to ...

A significant number of people had somehow managed to get ahead of me. I was slowing down. It turns out running gets harder the farther you go. My chest hurt. My legs hurt. My knees hurt. Oh, that's right. Running is the worst.

My ego had been stroked by the amount of people cheering me on though, so I decided, for the first time in my life, I would try at sport ... stuff. I at least wanted to finish, and not finish last. I was in pain, wanted to throw up, and knew unequivocally that this was not something I would ever put myself through again. So I pushed on, knowing it would be the last time, and somehow ended up coming third. (Out of about eleven people, but still – to me it was the equivalent of winning Wimbledon. Or whatever the most famous running thing is. The Super Bowl?)

When you come third, you get a ribbon, which was the first time I'd ever won a prize for anything non-academic in my life. I decided it was the perfect time to retire a champion. Knowing it was the last time I would ever have to do it was the only thing that motivated me to get to the end. I was done.

Then I was informed that the top three runners were required to represent the school in the 'regional' cross-country, a race that included about two hundred of the fastest kids from the entire Blue Mountains region.

Well, shit.

There was a lot of chatter about how the other talented athletes and I would go at 'regionals'. It sounded like it was going to be a high-pressure situation, which I had zero interest in. But it was imperative that we represent our primary school and represent it well – that's why the runners with the most talent had been chosen. Only the 'best of the best' went to regionals, obviously. Oh, and another thing, regionals wasn't three kilometres, it was five. But that'll be easy for the best runners, right?

I had almost puked up a lung as I crossed that three-kilometre finish line. This was not going to end well.

The regionals were being held at my sister's high school about half an hour away, so we could run the cross-country on a fancy running track because we were all very talented, fancy runners. I could get the bus in with Rhiannon, but I was going to need someone to come and pick me up, unless I wanted to wait four hours to get the high-school bus home. When I told Mum and Brian this, they responded just the way I had expected.

Mum was not exactly partial to the child pick-up. If we were old enough to read, we were old enough to get around without her having to sober up and drive somewhere to get us. It wasn't unusual to wait over two hours for her to arrive somewhere, if she arrived at all. In the days before mobile phones, we would have to call the house via a payphone, which we never had money for, so we would use reverse charges, which Mum never accepted. The only way you could hope to get a message to her would be to try and scam the reverse charge system. Our calls all ended up sounding something like this:

Phone recording: 'Hello. You have a caller requesting to speak to you via reverse charges. The caller's name is:'

Me: 'It'sRosieI'matthestationpleasescomeandgetme.'

Phone recording: 'If you would like to accept this call, please press 1. If not, you may hang up.'

She would always hang up. She usually turned up eventually. Usually.

I thought this was mostly normal. It wasn't until she made me go to a specialist doctor's appointment by myself when I was eleven years old that I realised my wandering the streets alone seemed to bother other adults. I had been getting pretty bad back pain for a while, and the local GP had sent me to get X-rays, which showed possible scoliosis. The GP referred me to a specialist at Westmead Children's Hospital, which was about an hour from where we lived in the Blue Mountains. I was pretty excited about this scoliosis thing, because I got to take the day off school and there was a KFC on the way back from Westmead, so I thought everything was coming up Rosie. The day came, however, and Mum didn't want to get out of bed.

'It's easy,' she said. 'Just catch the train. And there'll be maps at Westmead station directing you to the hospital. That whole bloody suburb is just the hospital. You can't miss it.'

I had caught the train to Penrith with my friends before so we could go to the movies, but this was different. To get to Westmead you had to change trains. And then I had to figure out where I was going. And then I had to talk to the doctor by myself. And then I had to figure out how to get the train home again. I just wanted a mum who drove their eleven-year-old daughters to stuff like this.

'Mum, just drive me. Please,' I said. 'I don't know what to say to the doctor!'

'Oh you'll be fine!' she said. 'He's just giving you the results of the X-ray, you don't have to say anything. And just call me from a payphone if you get lost. Reverse the charges!'

She wrote down the name and address of the doctor on the back of a used envelope, gave me money for the train and dropped me at the station.

When I got off the train at Westmead (after one incorrect attempt at changing trains that saw me head in the wrong direction for twenty minutes), I had no idea where to go. Despite Mum's assurances, the whole suburb wasn't 'just hospital'. I found a map on the station wall that pointed me in the right direction, but I just couldn't find this damn doctor's office. I kept looking at his name on the back of the envelope, hoping I was missing some crucial detail that explained why I couldn't find it. Like the next time I looked at it, I would say, 'Ohhh! His name is Peter, not John! I've been looking for John! No wonder I can't find it!' But I wasn't confused about the name. I was just lost. And my back hurt.

Not really knowing what to do, I finally found the main entrance of Westmead Children's Hospital, and approached the massive front desk. A friendly woman looked down at me. 'Hi, sweetie. Have you lost your parents?'

I wish.

'Um, no,' I said, clutching the envelope. 'I can't find the office I'm looking for. Can you tell me what floor it's on? My appointment is really soon.'

'Your appointment?' she asked, looking confused. 'You have an appointment? Just you?'

'Yeah I have an appointment with a specialist about my scoliosis. Do you know where this office is?'

I showed her the name and address.

'Oh. Sweetie. That doctor doesn't work out of the hospital. He has his own rooms in a building separate to the hospital. It's on this street but about ten minutes from here.'

I wanted to cry. I was so confused and Mum told me it was in the hospital and now I'm going to be late and I really don't want to walk for another ten minutes and why don't I have the kind of mum who just takes me to doctor's appointments and doesn't make me get the train and look stupid in front of this desk lady when I'M ONLY ELEVEN?

'Okay,' I said. 'Um, which way do I walk when I get outside?'

'When you walk out the doors, take a right,' she said. 'Good luck.'

I wandered up and down the street for another half an hour before I finally found the right building. The waiting room was filled with kids and teenagers, all sitting with their parents. And me.

The doctor called me in, and looked around the room when he saw only me get up. I walked straight into his office.

'Ah, is it just you today?' he asked, as he closed the door.

'My mum had to work,' I said quickly, picturing her currently lying in bed listening to 'Bitter Sweet Symphony' while on her second bottle of wine.

'Sit down, please,' he gestured. I had been awkwardly standing in the middle of the room. 'How did you get here? Did your mum drop you off?'

'No, um, I caught the train. And then walked from the station.'

'That's quite a long walk,' he said. 'I hope you didn't have to come far on the train?'

'Just from the Blue Mountains,' I replied, avoiding his eyes.

He stared at me in silence for a few seconds. Like there had been a glitch in the matrix in his office and his brain was trying to compute the nonsensical situation in front of him.

'Well, okay,' he finally said. 'Let's look at your X–rays, shall we?'

He told me that I had moderate scoliosis, and after that I have no idea what he said. I just kept smiling and nodding (exactly like I do now when someone talks about politics). He said something about a brace and physio and exercises and needing to see him again. Then he pulled out a voice recorder to say what he wanted his receptionist to type in my file. He started with, 'Patient Rosanna Waterland. Eleven years old. Rosanna has attended the appointment by herself today …' He suddenly stopped recording.

'Actually, I can finish recording this later,' he smiled. 'We're pretty much done here. Can you please ask your mum to call me? Just so we can go over your results and what needs to come next. Are you … Will you be okay getting home?'

'Yeah,' I said. 'I know the way now.'

It wasn't the worst thing my mum had made me do, by far, but there is nothing like knowing that the person you're talking to really pities you. That doctor, and the desk lady before him, really, really pitied me. And I felt like it was my fault. Like I just needed to act a little more confident. I just needed to look at the map a little more carefully. This whole thing wouldn't have looked as bad if I had just handled it better.

When I got back to my local station, I called Mum on the payphone ('It'sRosieI'matthestationpleasescomeandgetme'), and settled in for what would be at least an hour wait.

Considering I couldn't even get my mum to drive me to the doctor (and she never called him by the way, so here's hoping moderate scoliosis doesn't get progressively worse!), I wasn't hopeful that she or Brian would drive the one-hour round trip to pick me up after cross-country regionals. So not only was I doomed to humiliate myself by competing in a race I had no hope of finishing, I wasn't even sure how I was going to get home afterwards. This is why I never run.

Two hundred kids lined up at the starting line. All of them were stretching and wearing sweatbands and jogging on the spot. I was not a natural fit in such an environment. I was petrified of doing something stupid to reveal my ineptitude, like running in the opposite direction to everyone else when the gun went off. I just stood quietly, and tried not to make any sudden moves.

Then the time came. The gun went off, and everybody started running. I figured I could at least blend in for the first couple of hundred metres, but within about thirty seconds, I was lagging behind. And within about a minute, I was barely keeping up with the section of kids who were clearly there on some kind of special program. I think one of them may have been missing a leg. And he was beating me.

I was already exhausted, and I just wanted the whole thing to be over. I had been excited by my green ribbon, but this was just getting ridiculous now. I was not built to run. Plus, I really, really didn't want to. So, remembering that before the race, they told us medical attention would be available as needed throughout the course, I did the only thing I could think of to do.

'Fuck this,' I thought, and took a dive.

It wasn't a particularly convincing one, since I was scared I would hurt myself if I actually fell over for real. So basically one second I was running, and the next … I just sort of sat down. I fell dramatically into a comfortable sitting position, put my hand up, and waited for the medical staff.

A very enthusiastic young guy with a walkie-talkie made his way over to me. 'Hey! Are you okay? What's happened?'

I hadn't really thought of that.

'Oh … Um … Ow … My … Ankle? My ankle really hurts! I twisted it and then I fell! I heard a crack … sound, thing.'

'Can you take your shoe off?' he asked, reaching for my foot.

'OW! No! Please don't touch it! Um, ow! Oh, owww. I'm in so much pain.'

Now, I figured at this point he'd help me limp back to the starting line, then someone would call my mum or Brian, and given my horrific injuries, they'd have to come and pick me up. That way I'd get a lift home, and I'd be able to forever maintain that I was on track to win that race if it hadn't been for my damn injury. I would be the athlete that could have been a legend, if everything hadn't gone so horribly wrong.

Then things started to take a turn.

'Yeah, we're going to need the ambulance here,' enthusiastic young guy said into his walkie-talkie. 'Possible ankle fracture. At least a bad sprain. Student is in severe pain.'

Uh oh.

Within a few minutes, the ambulance showed up. They put me on a stretcher and loaded me in the back. This was all getting away from me very quickly. We then drove around the cross-country track, picking up other kids who had succumbed to injuries. There were about six of us sitting in the ambulance by the time we got back to the starting line. I studied their faces – I reckon about half of them had an 'injury' similar to mine. As in, a 'fuck this' injury.

Those kids were weak though. When the ambulance workers asked them if they were feeling better after sitting for a while, they sheepishly said yes and left. AMATEURS. I was committed to this. I was not saying I felt better until I knew someone was coming to pick me up.

'Oh! Owie. It hurts so much! The pain I am in! The pain!' I may have been overdoing it.

'Look, we're going to have to take these two to get checked out at the ER,' someone said, gesturing to me and a guy who actually looked really hurt.

Shit.

We were on our way to the hospital before I'd even had a chance to consider my options. This train had officially left the station. There was no turning back now.

It's very hard to explain to an ER doctor what is wrong with you when there isn't actually anything wrong with you. When they finally convinced me to take my shoe off (after I had to take a second to remember which foot I'd injured), they took one look at me and knew I'd caused barely, if any, actual damage during my 'fall'. The only indication that I'd hurt myself was my constant wailing that I'd hurt myself.

They wrapped the foot in a tight bandage, to discourage me from screaming in pain every time I moved it. Then they called my house, and about an hour later, Brian turned up and took me home, where I kept limping for two weeks, refusing to take the bandage off even when I showered, because I was committed to making the whole saga seem real. I'm not sure if anyone believed me. But those are the lengths I will go to, to avoid having to run. And getting that lift home was a bonus too.

Lifts from Brian were rare. That's why, when he offered to take me away from the house one night, I jumped at the chance.

I was about thirteen, and Mum had been drinking all afternoon. You knew it was bad when she started playing the same song over and over again on full-blast. Also when she started to make cruel comments about your face and/or general existence. Brian had copped the brunt of it that day, and by the time Mum was onto her third box of wine, he'd had enough. He needed to go to an all-night nursing shift in the city, so he decided to leave a little earlier just to get out of the house. He wouldn't be back until eight the next morning, and hopefully by then Mum would have turned back into Sober Lisa, who was actually quite a lovely person.

Brian asked me if I wanted to come with him. I could hang out at his work, watch TV and sleep in the nurses' station. 'C'mon, Rosanna,' he said. 'Don't stay here with her. She's just going to be like this all night.'

I could hear her randomly yelling something incoherent from the other room. I wanted to go with Brian, I really did. But Rhiannon had moved out, and both my little sisters were home. Tayla was five and Isabella was three. I couldn't leave them alone with Mum, could I?

It was only about 5pm; Mum still had a lot of drinking to do. I had spent countless nights like this with her in my life, and I had survived, but … That didn't mean it was okay to leave Tayla and Bella there, did it? They were just so little.

'Do you want to come or not?' Brian asked me.

I really, really wanted to go. I wanted to get the hell out of that house and as far away from Drunk Lisa as possible. Drunk Lisa made me anxious. Drunk Lisa gave me toxic butterflies.

I decided to leave. I reasoned if Brian thought it was okay for him to go, then it was okay for me to go too. I mean, he was the adult, right? I didn't really believe that though. I knew it was wrong to leave two little girls with my mum that night. I knew it was selfish. I knew that something awful could happen. But I still decided to leave. I just didn't want to be in that house. I was so tired.

I told Tayla to look after Bella, and that we'd be home in the morning. Then I walked out the front door and closed it behind me, leaving a five-year-old and a three-year-old to fend for themselves in a house with a woman who was so drunk she could barely stand.

I vividly remember sitting on the back of Brian's motorbike, staring through my helmet at the front door, knowing that something bad was going to happen. I just knew, as we drove away, that the life we had together in that house was never going to be the same.

And I still left.

When we returned home the next morning, the house was empty. During the night, Mum had decided to go out drinking with a friend, leaving Tayla and Bella home alone. Close to midnight, Bella came down with a fever. She was crying, and sick, and Tayla couldn't find anyone to help her. So, in what is one of the bravest things I've ever heard of a five-year-old kid doing, Tayla picked Bella up, took her out into the pitch-black night, and dragged her through the bush to the house next door. This was an isolated street in the Blue Mountains, not a busy neighbourhood – I used to be terrified walking around there at night, and I was thirteen. But Tayla knew she had to do something. She was the only person that night who knew she had to do something. She knocked on the door as hard as she could and waited for someone to answer. She just needed an adult, any adult, to help her sick little sister. She just needed someone to take care of her.

The neighbours answered. Police were called. Family services alerted. I was right – nothing was ever the same again. The night I left was the last night we would all live in that house together. I had broken the rules: our home life was meant to be a secret, and I had let the secret get out. Now we were caught.

All because I had left my little sisters alone.

I haven't had bad sex since I promised myself I wouldn't put up with it.
(Ha.)

Porn has broken the brains of men, and it is drying up the clits of women everywhere.

That's what was going through my head the night a man actually *spat in my face* because he thought it was sexy. Because porn had told him so. The seven-year-old me who accidentally figured out how to orgasm would weep for the current state of sexual affairs. What a tragedy.

I made a pact with myself, when I was about twenty-six, that I wasn't going to put up with crappy sex anymore. No more faking orgasms, no more pretending I was enjoying myself when I wasn't. The pleasure of the woman is just as important as the pleasure of the man, and I wasn't going to forget that. If I was allowing a peen to enter my vagina, then the owner of that peen had damn well better treat the experience like the absolute privilege that it is.

Unfortunately, this sexual pact with myself happened to coincide with the exact moment a lot of young men forgot how to have sex like real humans. And if you hook up with randoms for fun, as I am sometimes wont to do, then coming across one of these broken-brained men is par for the course. They have been brainwashed by porn. Pornwashed. I am living in an age of Pornwashed Millennials, and I'm not sure we can dial it back.

The first time I realised there was a serious problem was when I had a one-night stand with a 21-year-old. I was almost thirty. I'd never slept with someone that much younger than me before, but he was cute, and funny, and the party we were at was two streets away from my house, which was perfect for me because I really like penis and I really hate walking.

We made it into my bedroom, and did that awkward thing where you undress and wonder how the hell they do it so gracefully in the movies. Hands down, every single time I've had sex, there's been an awkward moment where the two of you have to split apart for a second to get some of your clothes off, especially shoes. I've never pulled off a 'start ripping off clothes in passion and continue taking them off each other seamlessly while walking to the bed at the same time' situation. I'm not entirely convinced it can be pulled off, actually. Just like sex standing up. Seriously – how do you angle the penis *upwards* into the vagina? That's how it works, right? Right? Oh god. I don't know anything. I never have. When my first boyfriend asked me if we could 'sixty-nine', not wanting to look clueless, I said 'sure thing' in my sexiest voice, then proceeded to thrust into him while counting to the number sixty-nine. He stopped me when I got to about fifteen, and said, 'No, Rosie, it's not… Well first of all you need to be facing the other way.' So I turned around, sat on him again, and kept counting.

Sufficiently naked and in bed, my new 21-year-old friend reached down to my lady garden and immediately pulled away, saying, 'Whoa.'

'What?' I said, in the panicked tones of someone whose genitalia just appeared to actually frighten a person.

'It's just, you've got a bush!' he said, giggling. 'I've never seen one.'

'Seriously?' I asked, although I wasn't really surprised by that. This was a conversation I'd had a few times. It would seem that most men of today expect a lady to have ripped her pubic hair out by the roots, in a painful procedure that leaves her looking like a pre-pubescent girl. I got a Brazilian wax once, as a surprise for my boyfriend at my high-school formal, and after experiencing what was possibly the worst pain of my entire life so far, I decided I would never put myself through that horror again. I let the hair grow back and kept it that way. I just figured it didn't bother *me*, so if I was ever going to remove it again, it would only be to please myself. And no way was I going through that kind of torture again for myself. My motto with men had always been, 'Well, if it bothers you, then kindly step away from my vagina.' I haven't had a guy step away yet.

I tried laser hair removal not long ago, because I'd spent years advocating my full-bush position, but so many women kept telling me that they didn't do it for men, they did it for themselves, because it felt 'cleaner', and I wanted to know if that was true. (I'm not sure if I believe that 'just for me' thing though, since I've heard many of the same women talk about the 'pubic hair chastity belt', which is the act of not removing one's pubic hair before a first date, so any temptation to sleep with said date is nipped in the bud. Because who would *ever* let a guy know they've hit puberty and have natural recurring female hormones AMIRIGHT LADEEZ?)

The pubic hair chastity belt is a mystery to me. The only thing stopping me from bringing a guy home is the amount of plates I have stacked next to my bed or the amount of empty bottles I may or may not have left in the bathroom (I highly recommend drinking chilled wine in the shower).

But I hadn't had a bald vagina since that one time when I was seventeen, so I thought I should try it again to see if maybe I liked it. I also knew that laser had become a thing, which I was told is not nearly as painful as ripping the hair out of your labia with hot wax. (Still painful, though, because 'no pain, no gain' AMIRIGHT LADEEZ?)

The girl at the laser clinic told me I would need to completely shave my entire pubic/bum region before coming in for my appointment. She apparently needed a zero-hair situation. No stubble, nothing. I nodded confidently, knowing full well there was no way I was going to be able to reach most of the places she just described. I hadn't reached those places in years. The fat upper pussy area maybe, but even then I would have to pull my belly back to make the skin taut enough to shave. (I am in the weird position of having lost a lot of weight, which means my body appears to have given birth to several children, when in fact my only child is my big screen TV called Gilda Radner, and the closest I've come to giving birth is pushing out a dump that felt like it was sitting horizontally across the inside of my poop hole.)

I didn't quite understand why I needed to shave off the hair that I was paying the clinic to get rid of, but the girl said some very impressive words about follicles and science, and I'm sure she'd been trained in a beauty school of some kind because she had very manicured eyebrows. So I trusted her advice, and went home to shave a bush I'd been growing since I was seventeen.

If you've ever tried bending over in the shower, pulling your bum cheeks apart with one hand while you reach up and in between your legs to shave your crack with the other, you may have some idea of what I spent my afternoon going through. I cannot even tell you the kind of pressure involved in trying to run a razor over some areas while narrowly avoiding others. Putting a razor anywhere near my labia and/or clitoris just doesn't feel natural to me. Like trying to go to the toilet outside – my body just freezes up and shuts down. I couldn't seem to build up the nerve required to shave close to any sensitive areas, which meant I ended up with a bald vagina that looked like it had just been through the careless, violent, patchy head-shaving that Anne Hathaway went through in that scene from *Les Miserables*. This was not a successful or aesthetically pleasing shaving job. And that was just the front – I have no idea what the back situation was like. I just closed my eyes, prayed to Oprah and tried to get as much of my bum as I could. It wasn't perfect, but damn it, it was the best I could do.

Apparently my best wasn't good enough, though. It's uncomfortable enough to have to get naked from the waist down, lie down on a table and spread your legs as far as they will go. But it's even worse when you do that and the heavily made-up technician looks directly into your snatch and lets out a big, unimpressed sigh.

'This is going to be difficult,' she said, wincing now but not looking away from my vag.

'What do you mean?' I asked. 'Did I miss a spot?'

'You missed most spots,' she said, putting her gloves on. 'Look, I can do this for you today, but the laser only works if there's no hair coming through the skin. So you're going to be … *patchy* until you come in for your next appointment. And next time, you really need to shave properly.'

She had said the word 'patchy' like she was describing a weeping sore on my vagina.

'It's just that, there were like, parts that I couldn't really reach,' I offered feebly. 'I thought I had got to most of it though.'

'Let's get started, shall we?' she snapped. She really wanted to get me out of that room. I was a hairy outsider who needed to be disposed of quickly, just in case she caught something. Like pubes were contagious.

The laser itself isn't really that painful. It just feels like someone is snapping a rubber band against your skin, but cool air is being blown onto the area at the same time, so you barely feel the sting before it's gone again. What was really off-putting was the smell of burning hair, which I suppose was my fault, for, you know, having some. It was only about halfway through the zapping that I started to consider the ramifications of allowing a laser that close to my clitoris. I'm no scientist, but I don't think we've been lasering our fish tacos long enough to know whether that thing causes lasting damage to the main bean. If a laser can cut through steel, then it sure as hell might be able to zap all the nerve endings out of a clitoris. I was just about to ask her if she knew of any studies that had looked into clitoral laser damage, but then we were done. The whole thing had taken about five minutes, if that.

'I'll just let you get dressed,' she said, rushing out of the room.

There is no doubt in my mind she was immediately going to tell the other technicians about the patchy freak show in Room 2. I know they say that they've seen it all and they're professionals and they would never talk about what goes on during hair removal, but if that was my job I can absolutely guarantee that I would be gossiping about weird-looking vaginas all day long. That would be the best part of the job.

I looked in the mirror before I put my pants on and was a little taken aback. My vag looked so ... bald. I didn't like it. It was shocking and a little wrong – like when you see Ron Swanson without a moustache. It just didn't look right. Plus, thanks to my fat upper pussy area, I didn't realise that the only thing stopping me from looking like I had two stomachs was the pubic hair. Now it just seemed like I had a top stomach and a bottom stomach with a little bit of labia sticking out between my thighs. But I was sexy and hairless, which is the main thing. (AMIRIGHT LADEEZ?) Well, I was sexy and hairless except for several small tufts that the razor hadn't reached, but that was as good as I could hope for.

The only other thing I noticed almost immediately was that my bum cheeks were slipping all over the place when I walked. I didn't realise that the pubes in my crack had been acting as a kind of non-slip buffer, stopping my crack sweat from sending my cheeks flying. I may have been hairless and sexy, but I spent the next few weeks with toilet paper wedged in my crack just to soak up moisture and hold everything in place.

I allowed the pubes to grow back. Getting rid of them didn't make me feel 'cleaner', I just felt … unrecognisable. It was like my vag and I didn't know each other anymore. And I like being familiar with what she's got going on, you know?

But when I was in bed with the 21-year-old hotshot, I still had my pubes and they were shocking to him. What should have been shocking was that he'd never seen a woman with pubic hair, but this is the time we live in.

He didn't fixate on the pubes for long though; they never do when penetration is on the table. And unfortunately, this penetration was over very quickly. This was how my new young friend did the sex (and I say 'did the sex' because I honestly feel like that was probably how he described it):

He got on top of me, thrust into me like a jackhammer, came, then he was done. Then he rolled off, gasping for air after his intense workout, and asked, 'So did you come?'

I wasn't even sure I'd blinked.

'Um, yes,' I said, unconvincingly. 'That was sooo great.'

I just didn't have the time or the inclination to educate the poor boy. He had clearly grown up watching the kind of porn where women are just heads attached to hairless vaginas, who scream in pleasure as soon as a penis even brushes up against them. That he thought I could have orgasmed from what he just did was gobsmacking to me. Porn had broken his brain. He was Pornwashed.

I sent him off into the night and left him to be some other woman's problem. I'm too old to be teaching men that having sex with a woman is more complicated than having sex with a Fleshlight that has a human body attached to it.

Soon after that … *tryst*, I came down with Glandular Fever. So rather than give me an orgasm, he gave me an illness that kept coming back for the better part of a year. I accepted it, though, as my punishment for not sending him back into the world with more skills than when I found him. Glandular Fever was my sexual karma, and I was paying the price. Which is why I couldn't believe it when a new guy I had met on Tinder spat in my damn face. WASN'T GLANDULAR FEVER PUNISHMENT ENOUGH, OH OPRAH?

Tinder is a strange place. The very first time I used it, in less than twenty-four hours I ended up in a game of Jenga with my face and a penis. Naturally, I promised myself I would never return, and I didn't, for about a year. Then I caved. Going back on Tinder after a while is like finally finding something new in the fridge after opening it a million times and seeing nothing but the fresh vegetables that have liquefied because you bought them while feeling motivated but kept eating chicken nuggets instead. After a year, it seemed like the Tinder fridge was full again. But it only took me about a day to realise that the fridge was full of the same rotting, liquefied vegetables that were there all along.

Online dating seems to have a bizarre effect on some men, causing them to behave in ways that would be considered psychotic, pervy or even criminal in real life. Dating apps, especially, are like the Superman phonebox for a lot of guys – they step in as their normal, seemingly decent selves, and step out asking every woman on the street if she would like to be sprayed with jizz.

Why do so many men feel like the online world is different to the real world? Why do the rules of general decency go out the window as soon as they log in to a dating app? In order to explain to men how bizarre this behaviour actually is, it's much easier to look at it as if it were, in fact, happening in the 'real world'. Because if men behaved in real life like they do on online dating sites, they would find themselves in situations like this:

See a woman you like in a bar. Introduce yourself by cupping your penis in your hand and proudly presenting it to her. If she does not appreciate your penis, scream at the top of your lungs that she is a 'fat cunt bitch'.

See a woman you like in a bar. Say hi. If she responds, immediately assume she is desperate to have sex with you and demand to see her nipples. Sit back and wait for her inevitable orgasm.

See a woman you like in a bar. Walk up behind her and whisper in her ear that you are masturbating that very second. If she ignores you, do the exact same thing to the next woman you come across.

See a woman you like in a bar. Don't say hello. Don't introduce yourself. Just sit down at her table and tell her how much you'd like to feel her big toe up your bum hole.

See a woman you like in a bar. Have a lovely twenty-minute conversation with her, at which point you announce that you've invested enough time and now deserve a peek at her vagina. Or at least one tit.

See a woman you like in a bar. See more women you like in that bar. In fact, just like every woman in the bar and keep showing them all your penis. It's a numbers game, after all.

See a woman you like in a bar. Say hi. Get no response. Say hi again. Get no response. Call her a fucking ugly slut who deserves to die. If she finally responds and says she didn't hear you the first time, ask if maybe she'd like to hang out some time.

See a woman you like in a bar. Shake her hand. Smile and say you just jerked off with those fingers.

See a woman you like in a bar. Refuse to engage with her until she tells you about her pubic hair situation. Actually, just wear a sign around your neck that says 'Bald Vag Only'. That should save time.

See a woman you like in a bar. Approach her and tell her that you'd love to get her off. When she responds that she'd actually love for you to touch her clit, freak the fuck out and quickly google its location.

See a woman you like in a bar. Ask her if the carpets match the drapes. Bask in the brilliance of your hilarious pick-up line and wait for her to undress.

See a woman you like in a bar. Get a closer look at her face and tell her you'll fuck her, but only from behind.

See a woman you like in a bar. Ask her about her hopes and dreams. Listen intently. When she asks you yours, say, 'To have you riding my dick by the end of tonight.'

See a woman you like in a bar. Approach her and introduce yourself. Ask her about her life and listen when she responds. See if she'd maybe like to meet up for a drink sometime. Struggle to understand when she thanks you for not taking your dick out and shoving it in her face.

It's no wonder that when a man behaves like a normal human being while online, it suddenly feels very impressive. Like chivalry was dead, and by not immediately asking to see your 'wet pussy', he has brought it back to life. For a man to be considered a 'catch' online these days, he just has to not be disgusting. That is the new base level of acceptable man.

That's how it feels when you're online dating, anyway. So when I came across a guy who just wanted to chat about TV and laugh about memes, I was … cautiously optimistic. Then we realised we were watching the same TV show at the same time, so we started trying to outdo each other with jokes (I won, obviously). Then we realised that we lived right around the corner from each other, and he suggested that he come over, and we watch TV together. He would even pick up gelato on the way! I liked the sound of all of that. It really is my dream for all dates to involve watching TV at home while eating gelato, so I told him to come on over.

I had not planned on having sex with this person, but there was some wine involved, which meant I was very romanced by the TV and gelato. So when he leaned over to kiss me and we started making out, I thought, 'Yeah, okay, he brought gelato, I'm into this.'

It seemed normal at first. Normal making out during a normal make-out session on a normal couch in my normal apartment. Very, very normal.

Then we went to the bedroom, and the full extent of this guy's Pornwashing became apparent.

It was subtle at first. When we started having sex, he was on top of me, and he asked if he could slap my bum. 'Sure,' I said. I liked that he asked, and don't mind a bit of a slap during sex anyway. Then he asked if he could do it a little harder. Okay. Well, he's asking. 'Sure, go a little har—'

'YOU LIKE THAT, YOU FUCKING BITCH, DON'T YOU?'

Wait, whaaaat?

'Um, yes?' I said, a little thrown by that outburst, but not thrown enough to stop. I was more fascinated, to be honest, so I decided to keep going.

'Hey, is this okay?' he asked, as he put his hands around my neck and applied a little pressure.

I didn't feel threatened at all, just … bewildered. But I'm open to new stuff, and he was still asking before he did anything that might make me uncomfortable, so I figured I'd give it a go.

'Can I apply more pressure?' he asked about a minute later.

'Uh, sure,' I said, studying his face now like it was a science exhibit. His eyes were tightly closed, he was thrusting in and out of me, and so far all he'd asked me was if he could do a few very specific things that he clearly needed to be turned on – slapping me, choking me and calling me a fucking bitch. It was like he was masturbating, and I was just one of many tools that he was using to get the job done.

And as I lay there, being bounced around underneath him, I was still just so *fascinated*. I was witnessing the sad results of Pornwashing in real time! I was like a sexual David Attenborough! I was a selfless anthropologist, being penetrated so I could take a detailed look into what men think sex is like after being raised on porn. My date seemed to be struggling now. His face was sweating and the thrusting was getting faster. He had one hand around my neck and was using the other to slap my thigh, but it just didn't seem like it was getting him there.

And just as I was wondering what messed-up thing he might ask me to do in order to help him come, he did it.

All of a sudden, he looked right into my eyes ... and SPAT ON MY FACE.

He spat. On my face. And the sound he made as he was doing it made it obvious that he'd come.

He rolled off me, breathing heavily.

I was pissed off.

'Um, did you just fucking spit on me?' I asked.

'Oh, yeah,' he said, giggling. 'Sorry. Normally I ask – getting permission is *really* important to me, but I was just so close, it got away from me a bit.'

Bullshit. He knew I wouldn't say yes to having my face spat on, so he just did it. And now he was trying to justify it by indicating that he was a good guy, because he'd asked about the other stuff.

BULL. SHIT.

It should also be pointed out here that at no point so far had he asked me about my pleasure. This entire twenty-minute session had been about him satisfying his sexual needs. And his needs were messed up – anybody who needs to slap a girl, choke a girl, call her a fucking bitch and then spit in her face just to be able to orgasm, is broken. That person's brain is broken. I will say though, that while the very unexpected spitting did make me feel a little violated, I wasn't scarred by it in any way. I didn't feel assaulted or abused — if I had felt that way, I would have said so. I made it clear that I thought the spitting was gross and that he shouldn't have done it. But I was mostly just annoyed that the sexual experience as a whole had been so … *unsatisfying*.

I'm not sure whether he didn't ask me what *I* needed to get off because he was selfish, or if he'd watched so much porn that it just didn't occur to him that my needs were even an issue. I suspect the latter.

I asked him to leave. I kept the gelato.

Porn really has broken the brains of men. (Okay, fine — NOT ALL MEN.) I'm a lot more outspoken these days about what I will and won't accept in the bedroom, but the epidemic of Pornwashing out there means I'm bound to occasionally come across a dud who just does not know how to pleasure a woman. I like sex, so I just can't beat those odds.

But I'm not going to maintain a bald vagina, or pretend I enjoy getting jackhammered just because that's the only way he can get his penis to work now. His weird porn habits are his problem, and I have enough to deal with already.

Women currently have to navigate their way through a sexual universe of very, very confused dicks. It's tough out there.

Good luck to us all in our quest for orgasms.

It took longer than I expected to get Tony's body home from Austin. Although his friends there had confirmed it was him, he needed to be formally identified by a family member before his body could be released. He had cousins in Chicago who flew to Austin to complete the difficult task, before making the long journey home with him to Griffith.

He died on July 7th, and because of the difficulty in getting him home, the funeral wasn't scheduled until July 23rd. It was such an odd period of time. Like a grief waiting room. Constantly being on the precipice of exploding emotion, but having to keep it in a jar until the exact right moment. I could see the pain and adrenalin through the glass; I knew it was there. I would poke holes in the lid and let little bits out, but it somehow seemed like the worst was yet to come. The lid was going to have to come off. I knew it was coming. And I just had to sit with it.

I went back to Sydney for a few days, to be with my sisters and to visit the apartment Tony and I had shared together. I thought it would make me feel closer to him, but it just felt ... wrong. So wrong.

My younger sister Tayla had taken over the lease after I went to Melbourne and Tony went to Austin, so a lot of the same furniture was there, a lot of Tony's pictures were still on the walls, the hipster light fixtures he had bought from Kmart hung from all the ceilings. But it wasn't the same. I think I had hoped to walk into that apartment and see the home Tony and I had shared. Maybe even see Tony, waiting for me on the couch with a glass of wine, ready to watch *RuPaul's Drag Race*. But all I saw was something that looked the same, but wasn't. Like visiting a place you loved as a child, and not being able to recapture its magic. It wasn't our home. It looked like it from the outside, but the inside was hollow. It wasn't our home.

I was lost. Melbourne didn't feel like right, and now Sydney didn't feel right either. I had come to Sydney to chase down a warm, familiar feeling, but it wasn't there. So I flew back to Melbourne, which felt just as wrong. I was starting to drift off into space, and I kept reaching out for Tony, but he wasn't there to grab my hand. What was I supposed to do when he didn't grab it? I had no idea, so I just kept floating further and further away. I shut myself in my apartment, and never left. Jacob would ask me if I needed him to come over, and I would say no. I didn't want to talk to anybody anymore. I couldn't risk the lid coming off. I just needed to be numb.

More TV, more drinking, more dissociating. Not showering. Not changing clothes. Ordering food in. Never opening the blinds. Dishes piling up. Cat poo filling the litter tray. I knew I wasn't handling things well, but I just figured I needed to make it to the funeral. That would bring closure. That would bring the release I'd need to smash the lid off everything and move on. After the funeral, things would be better. I just needed to make it to the funeral.

Tony's sister, Sarina, had asked me if I would give Tony's eulogy with his oldest and dearest friend, Assunta. Initially, I was grateful for something to concentrate on, but soon found whatever writing talent I may have once had, had disappeared off the planet with Tony. My brain was broken. Closed for business. Not unlike my vagina when I first tried to put tampons in it. Everything completely locked up. I only seemed capable of watching TV and getting drunk. I certainly couldn't think about Tony being gone, and definitely couldn't write anything that would come close to summing up his entire, brilliant life.

But I was the professional writer. Tony had made sure of that. So I told Sarina and Assunta to send me their notes, and I promised to put something incredible together. I didn't know how, since I could barely function enough to clean myself, but after everything Tony had done to push me into the writing career I had always dreamed of, the least I could do was put down the vodka, pull my head away from the TV and write something that would do his life justice.

Then I started obsessing about the door. That damn door.

The door was the last thing that I was ever annoyed at Tony about. Basically, the situation was this:

Our Sydney apartment was at least fifty years old. At least. Our lovely landlord John sometimes told us stories about tenants he had in the 1960s and '70s, so the building had been around a long time.

So, the apartment, though lovely, was a very old design, and had a door between the living room and the hallway that led to the bedrooms. It was such an odd place for a door – if you shut all the bedroom doors and the living room door, you had basically just shut yourself into a bizarre closet-like space. And, the weird door opened *into* the living room, which got in the way all the time, so one day I finally decided that I would just take it down. I carefully unscrewed the hinges, placed them in a little plastic bag along with all the screws, and taped the bag to one side of the door. That way, it could easily be put back on if and when we ever moved out. John was a great landlord, and I didn't want to damage the place in any way. I put the door into the backroom and didn't really think about it again.

Until.

About six months later, I was living in Melbourne, Tony was in Austin, and my little sister Tayla had an inspection at the Sydney apartment. Within a few days, she got an email from the real estate agent, who wanted to know where the door from the living room was. Tayla called me.

'Oh yeah,' I said. 'I took that down when I put those bookshelves in the living room. It was just getting in the way. But don't stress – it's in the backroom. Just email them and tell them that we still have it, and we'll put it back on if we ever move out.'

Tayla called me back five minutes later. 'Rosie, it's not in the backroom.'

'Tayla,' I responded, patronisingly, 'yes, it is. You just didn't look properly. I put it in there with a little bag filled with the hinges and screws taped to it. I don't know how you could miss it. I mean, it's a door.'

'I wouldn't miss it, Rosie. It's not there. There is no door in the backroom.'

Still I didn't believe her. There is no way an entire door could just disappear. I demanded that she photograph the entire backroom and send me the pictures. She did. She also sent me a video, and I was sure she was giving me the finger just out of shot.

There was no door in the backroom.

'I don't get it!' I said to Tayla. 'It's a whole fucking door. What happens to a door? You know what? It has to be Tony. I bet Tony did something weird with it for some random Instagram photo or something. Let me call him.'

I called Tony in Austin.

'Sup mamasitaaaa!' he said, answering the phone.

I launched right into it. I was in no mood.

'Hey, Tonz, remember how I took the door off the hinges in the living room to make more space for the bookshelves?'

There was silence on the other end of the line. That was always the first sign Tony was fibbing about something – momentary panicked silence. I could imagine the exact look on his face.

'Um ... no? What door?' he responded.

FIRST MISTAKE. I knew he knew about the door, because we had had many conversations about the door, and he had talked about how much better the living room looked without the door, so telling me now that he doesn't even remember the door was obviously a lie, because I knew he knew about the door. And he knew that I knew he knew. He was busted.

'Tonz. I know you know about the door.'

'I mean, I think, yeah,' he stammered. 'The door. That living room door, right? I can't even remember if it was there or not when I went to Austin.'

SECOND MISTAKE. He was freaking out now and doubling down on the lie.

'Antonio. There are shelves where the door used to be, so unless the shelves were gone, there's no way the door could have been there. Were the shelves gone?'

'Um ...'

'Listen,' I said, trying to play good cop now. 'Did you maybe do something with the door? Like, use it for a photoshoot or something? Or let one of your friends use it for a production? I don't care, Tonz, I don't. I mean obviously the door is gone. But I just need to know. It can't have just disappeared.'

'Shit, Ro, I have to go! I'll call you back!'

THIRD MISTAKE. He did not call back. He was avoiding me, I'm sure in an attempt to buy time and come up with a story.

I messaged him for days about that damn door, even though I knew from his first panicked response that he was never going to tell me anything. In the end, I was just begging him to tell me *something*, because the mystery of the whole thing was driving me crazy. I NEEDED TO KNOW.

After a tortuous dinner with Jacob, in which I forced him to listen to an hour-long analysis of the door conspiracy being spearheaded by Tony from the other side of the world, Jacob told me I really needed to let go of the door. And I did, mostly, but the mystery continued to eat away at me.

And in the days I was meant to be writing the eulogy, my obsession with the door came back with a vengeance. What had Tony done with it? Did he throw it out to make more space? Did he give it to someone? Did he use it for some convoluted photo on Instagram? Is the backroom of the Sydney apartment the storage equivalent of the Bermuda Triangle? Had the door simply ... *disappeared*?

The door is what I thought about instead of Tony's life, which I was meant to be condensing into the most beautiful and moving thing Assunta and I would ever read.

That damn door.

The night before my sisters and I were going to drive to Griffith for the funeral, I still hadn't written a word. I spent the night on Rhiannon's couch, playing with my nephew Mohammed and avoiding doing what needed to be done. The funeral was still two days away, but Sarina and Assunta obviously needed to read what I had written before then, so that any changes could be made. He was their family, and this was for them – they needed to see what I'd written. I knew I couldn't arrive in Griffith the night before the funeral without having it done, so I sat in Rhiannon's living room, frozen in fear until 4am. Then I started writing.

It was done in less than two hours; it flowed out of me, even though I didn't want it to. It was both the hardest and easiest thing I'd ever written.

When I was done, I sat for a long time, staring at my desktop. I couldn't believe there was a file on it that said 'Antonio Sergi – A Eulogy'.

ANTONIO PAUL SERGI: A EULOGY
To be read by Assunta

Antonio, T-Buff, Tonz, Tony, T, was born here, in Griffith, on December 16th, 1986, to his incredibly loving parents, Pat and Maria. The baby of the family and a star from the very beginning, his three older siblings, Frank, Sarina and Joseph, were pushed out of the spotlight the day he arrived. Antonio was not meant to be anywhere but centre stage, and without even trying, the spotlight was always his.

He was a heartbreakingly gorgeous little boy, with huge brown eyes and an infectious laugh that he carried with him into adulthood. Leave him alone for five minutes and he would be performing to an imaginary audience – usually some dramatic scene from a movie in which he'd play all the parts. Or he'd be starring in a concert, with Sasha the family dog forced to sit front row. Obviously, Tony knew that to be front row at one of his many concerts was an honour that Sasha was lucky to have.

As well as a passion for performance and a charisma that had the capacity to light up any dark space, the other quality that shone through in Tony from an early age was his kindness. His absolute generosity of spirit when it came to the people he loved. It's unusual for a child so young to be so selfless, but Antonio was just beginning a life in which he would give his love freely, to anyone who needed it. His heart would only grow bigger as he did, and this was never more clear than in his ability to make every friend he had feel like the most important person in the world. Actually, as Tony would say (usually while holding a crystal) – not just the world, but the universe.

From primary school, right through to high school, he was forming lifelong bonds. He was unique, even back then, and those like myself, who found friendship with him so early on, knew how lucky we were to have him. There was nothing quite like having an emotional conversation with T-Buff about Sarah Michelle Gellar's brilliant performance on *Buffy* the night before. And we would usually have that conversation while wagging at Maccas instead of going to PE. And his love of television did not stop at *Buffy*. Antonio may be one of the only people on earth to become so invested in *The Real Housewives of New Jersey* that it would actually make him cry. You always knew, when he said he was going to his room to 'watch his stories', that he was going to be emotional for at least a few hours. But as invested as he was in every reality TV show he could find, Antonio always said that his own life would make a better one. And he was probably right.

As strong as his school friendships were, though, Antonio was not the type of guy to pick friends over family. Family was everything to him. He was a best friend and confidant to all of us. It's no surprise that Tony was asked to plan most family events and MC at pretty much everybody's weddings and birthdays – he was the favourite of every person sitting here today. Tony was the person in the family you would call. The person who would listen. His brain was like a computer when it came to the personal details of all of our lives. Who in here hasn't called Tony at some point, and talked to him for an hour about that random person who's been annoying you, because you know that Tony's the only one who is completely up-to-date with every detail of the drama? Who hasn't had him over for late-night pizza to talk about a break-up, always when you were both meant to be dieting? Those nights, filled with endless laughter, are now memories we can cherish always.

Every woman in Tony's family was his sister. Every man his brother. His nieces and nephews, whom he loved even more than Buffy, were like children to him. Francesca, Joseph, Marissa and Patrick were the magic in his life. His mother, Maria, shared a bond with him that is rare to find between mother and son these days. They were still going on date nights to the movies just this year. Hearing the two of them giggling together was to hear true love.

And Antonio's heart was just so filled with love. They say that we each have only one soulmate. Not Antonio. Antonio has left behind more soulmates than anyone ever has. We were all the great loves of Antonio's life. From his family the day he came home from the hospital, a tiny newborn, to the new friends he was making just weeks ago in Austin, Tony had this incredible skill – he made everybody feel like they were his best friend. His soulmate.

Antonio made you feel like his heart was filled with love just for you. And that's because it was. Antonio Sergi's heart was infinite. It could be filled with love, and then filled again and again and again. He loved each person sitting here today like only a person with an infinite heart could. There was space in there for all of us.

To be read by Rosie

Antonio was also an unstoppable force. Something about him was electric. And he always knew it too. He knew his life was going to be bigger than Griffith. He knew he was going to explore the world and live his dreams. He had grown up watching the three TV channels Griffith had to offer, and he was going to end up on one of them. So at just eighteen, he moved to Sydney on his own, and started at drama school.

His skill for comedy made him an immediate star. His obsession with *Saturday Night Live* and Tina Fey meant he schooled us all in improv before we even knew what it was.

This is also, unfortunately, the time when Tony finally, after a lifetime of hoping and trying, had to accept that he was a really, really bad singer. I loved him, but I have never met someone whose level of desperation to be able to sing was only matched by how terrible he was at it. That did not stop him, though. There can't be one person in this room who hasn't heard him belt out a very unique version of

'Part of Your World' from *The Little Mermaid*. Tony secretly confessed to me, just before his tonsil surgery a few months ago, that he was praying that when he woke up, he'd have a flawless singing voice. He also confessed that may have been the main reason he asked his parents for the surgery in the first place. Antonio was never going to give up on a dream.

Drama school was also where Tony began to grow into an adult. His spectacular sense of style began to take shape. Let's be honest – nobody will ever rock a crystal necklace, a bow tie and an old '80s blazer from Maria's closet quite like Antonio Sergi. He never had a hair out of place, and his ability to fall into a model pose whenever a camera pointed in his direction was unmatched. He didn't have the beard yet when I first met him, although I have to say I agree with his nonna on that one – it just hid his beautiful face.

When drama school ended, most in our class let their acting dreams go, in favour of seeking out a 'grown-up' life. Not Tony. He was determined, and he knew his path. He went on to more intensive study of drama, turning his diploma into a Bachelor of Arts degree. He then went on to obtain a Masters in Media Arts and Production from the University of Technology in Sydney, and the University of Texas in Austin. And Tony didn't just graduate – he kicked arse. His Masters degree, a very rare thing to get anyway, came with a High Distinction average and a grade point average of 4.0. That's basically like the Academy Award equivalent of grades. Antonio had found his calling – he was brilliant at producing. It can be seen in some of the work he created over the last few years, from his beautiful short film about his Aunt Julie, which was selected for a film festival, to his creation of his Rosie Runs videos. I may have hated him for forcing me to exercise, but those videos – entirely his creation from the initial idea to the final edit – have now been seen by over two million people.

And while we're on the subject of Tony's ability to produce incredible images, we obviously need to take a moment to honour his Instagram, a perfectly curated piece of art. You can actually pinpoint the moment he decided Instagram stardom was going to be his, as his feed went from unflattering selfies to *Vogue*-style photos within twenty-four hours. I would often tease him when he sat on the couch in our apartment, a plate of microwaved Griffith salami sitting next to him, while he spent hours – literally, hours – editing a single photo before it was ready to be released to the world. He once forced me to take one hundred and fifty-seven shots of him holding a milkshake. But I'm so glad now that he did, because his Instagram feed is such a stunning visual tribute to his life. Particularly to his travels, which he had so enjoyed the last couple of years. His time in Austin was some of the happiest in his life. He always felt a special connection with America, and that he got to spend so much time there, with a whole new tribe of soulmates, is so lovely to know.

But Tony always loved to come home. A Griffith boy will always be a Griffith boy. He was so excited to attend Joseph's wedding to Melissa in September. Of course, he was the fashion genius who had picked the dress, and there was no way he was going to miss his flawless choice walking down the aisle. He had invited me as his date, since he had always told me that I would not BELIEVE what a real Griffith Italian wedding was like. He was so looking forward to it blowing my mind. It was one of his dreams, actually, to come back to Griffith one day and make a reality show about the Italian wedding scene. I think we all know he would have done it too.

Because that's the type of man Antonio was. He spent his twenty-nine years on this earth doing two things – loving everyone in his life unconditionally, and following his creative dreams.

Antonio was electric. Antonio had an infinite heart. He was hilarious. He was creatively brilliant. He was selfless. He was generous. He was stylish. He was so good looking. He was TV-obsessed. He was an academic Master. He was an unstoppable force. He was love. Antonio was just walking, talking love.

And because he loved each of us so much, Antonio wouldn't want us to cry as we say goodbye. He wouldn't want his passing to cause pain. He wouldn't want us to let the darkness of loss take over.

But there *is* something, as a lifelong performer, that he would want. And since his greatest performance ended up being his extraordinary life, it is something that he deserves. So I am honoured, as one of his many, many soulmates, to ask you all now, to please give Antonio Paul Sergi a round of applause.

I attached the file to an email and sent it off to Tony's sister in Griffith. As of that morning, it was the only thing I'd ever written that Tony hadn't read.

And I still hadn't figured out what he did with that damn door.

I was very briefly possessed by the Devil.
(Look, I probably wasn't, but I don't think this one can be verified either way.)

When I was about five years old, my dad let me watch Stephen King's horror movie *IT*. I don't know if he wanted to watch it and my older sister and I just happened to be there, or if he specifically thought it would be an interesting experiment of human nature to see how two little girls react to being traumatised by a clown who eats children. (Given the way he liked to torment us in other ways, I suspect the latter. He once spent an entire day telling Rhiannon and me in secret that he loved each of us more than the other. Obviously, we proudly told each other the news that we were 'Daddy's Favourite', because as a pre-schooler that means you have won at everything that could ever possibly matter. Then he would laugh hysterically as we had what was no doubt an adorable screaming match, because a four-year-old and a six-year-old in an emotional battle over their father's love must have been hilarious.) Either way, like many kids my age in the early 1990s, I saw the movie and it scarred me for life. It also led to my bizarre, abusive relationship with horror films, which peaked with me crying on the phone to my mother after watching *The Exorcist*, convinced that my body had been possessed by the Devil.

But it all started with Pennywise the Dancing Clown.

Rhiannon and I were visiting my dad at a halfway house in Wollongong, during one of his very brief stints as a 'sober' person. We lived in Sydney with Mum, so he would catch the train from Wollongong to Central Station in the city, where we would meet him and jump on the train before it went back to Wollongong. This happened every weekend for a couple of months. After settling us on the train, he would always leave us in our seats to go and buy our favourite treats from the shop at the station – a spring roll for Rhiannon and a fried chicken drumstick for me. I could never understand why he would risk missing the train like that. I remember being so anxious, watching the clock count down to departure time, with Dad nowhere in sight. I didn't need the damn drumstick – I just didn't want to be left alone on the train to Wollongong. But he always jumped through the doors just as they were closing, drumstick for me, spring roll for Rhiannon, and the definite smell of alcohol on his breath. I knew that smell well.

The halfway house was exactly the kind of place you imagine people would go after getting out of prison or rehab. Kind of like a university share-house, but filled with men in recovery instead of students. So, the epitome of fun for two little girls. I didn't mind that it was all men really, or that I didn't know them — my sister and I had been living in random share-houses with Mum since we were born. We had been raised in the 'this is your home now, make the best of it' school of childrearing. I was used to forced familiarity with whoever we needed to split the rent. At least the men sharing with Dad in this place were nice. And I knew he wasn't allowed to drink around them, so it was actually one of the only times I ever felt safe spending time with my dad.

A young guy with long hair had a Gameboy that he let me play, which I just thought was the most incredible thing to have ever happened in my entire life. We had a Nintendo at home that we played Mario Brothers and Duck Hunt on, but that had to be plugged into the TV. This guy could take his Nintendo with him, anywhere he wanted, ALL THE TIME. That was some Jetsons-level technology. That he couldn't be more than twenty-two and was living in a halfway house for addicts and felons meant nothing to me — he could play Mario on the toilet. I couldn't imagine a more glamorous life.

In the room next to the young guy was an Aboriginal man who was an incredible artist. He used to let Rhiannon and me use his charcoal to draw pictures that he would hang up next to his, like we were proper artists too. It was obvious he liked Rhiannon a lot more than me because she actually had some artistic talent. I had what could be described as an 'awww, you did a little drawing' level of talent. He used to encourage us to find beauty in the everyday things around us, so Rhiannon would sketch these incredible still-lifes of the TV stand or the plant on the balcony. She was only eight years old, the bitch. I did what I have continued to do in my adult life when I can tell I'm not good at something that I really wish I was good at – retreated into immature humour because 'IT'S DUMB ANYWAY'. I would draw pictures of Rhiannon's face covered in pimples and with monster teeth because art is dumb and I hate it and you smell. I like to think it's just as charming when I behave that way now as it was back when I was five.

I'm not entirely clear on how the screening of *IT* began. But I can remember sitting in the living room with my dad, Rhiannon and his two flatmates, and being nervous about what I was going to see, but trying to act cool. Like, yeah, I'm five, but I can totally handle Georgie getting pulled down into the sewer, where my dad helpfully informed me his arm had been ripped off, because they don't make that clear in the movie.

I had seen one horror film before, called *Night of the Living Dead*, also with my dad. I can't have been more than about three years old, but that movie is burned into my brain. Rhiannon and

I were sharing a bed then, and I stayed up all night, staring into her sleeping face, convinced she was going to wake up and eat my brains. I kept looking around the room for weapons, and had decided on the lamp, which looked like the only thing sturdy enough to take her down.

I can just see the headlines now: '3-year-old girl murders 6-year-old sister with lamp. What turned this sweetheart into a killer?' (Or the *Daily Mail* version – 'SCANTILY CLAD 3-YEAR-OLD IN REVEALING CARE BEARS NIGHTIE SAVAGELY MURDERS INNOCENT SISTER IN WHAT APPEARS TO BE A RITUALISTIC KILLING WITH SATANIC UNDERTONES. POLICE NOT RULING OUT JEALOUS ROW OVER MUTUAL CRUSH – ATREYU FROM "THE NEVER ENDING STORY". WAS HE THE LOVER OF THEM BOTH? WE SPECUALTE ON THAT AND MORE.'

When I woke up in the morning, Dad had moved us both to the couch, because I had thrown up in the bed, which I can only assume was from unbearable fear (of having my brains eaten and also of unfairly spending my life in prison for defending myself against a horrifying sister zombie). Rhiannon is thirty-three now, and I still can't look at her sleeping face without thinking about her shoving a handful of my brain tissue into her mouth. I also always quickly scan the room for possible weapons.

Despite having thrown up after *Night of the Living Dead*, I sat through the entire *IT* telemovie. Both parts. IT killing the little girl on the bike. The guy writing 'IT' in blood on the bathroom wall. Balloons popping blood into people's faces. IT coming up through the shower drain. IT's hand bursting out of the photo album. The giant, nonsensical spider.

I couldn't sleep for weeks. Months. Maybe even years. The amount of nightmares I had about that clown is sickening. I couldn't walk past a drain without thinking he was going to pull me down and rip my arm off. But, for some inexplicable reason, I kept going back for more. *IT* had awakened something in me, and now I wanted all the horror movies, all the time. *Candyman. A Nightmare on Elm Street. Child's Play. Friday the 13th. Halloween. Poltergeist.* I couldn't stop. I would torture myself watching these things, and then torture myself even more by living a life of terror in which I couldn't sleep or be alone without thinking about all the possible ways I could be murdered.

I suppose my mum could have stepped in at some point, but she was often the one renting the movies for me, since even the most lax, pimply, video-store worker felt strange about handing over a copy of *The Texas Chainsaw Massacre* to a seven-year-old. 'Oh,' Mum would say, barely looking at the box. 'Is that the one you want? Are you sure? Well you're not bloody sleeping in my bed again, I'm telling you right now.'

Yet there I'd be, at 2am, creeping into her room with my blanket, happy to just sleep on the floor next to her bed, because everybody knows that parents have a bubble of murder immunity around them. As long as I was in her room, I was safe. Even if she was drunk out of her mind and listening to Elton John while snot crying, the Candyman couldn't get me in there. Not according to my logic, anyway.

I once forced her to stand outside the bathroom with a butcher's knife while I went to the toilet, because I didn't feel I could guarantee my own safety. 'You're being ridiculous, Rosanna,' she said. 'I'm not bloody doing it.'

'You don't understand!' I cried. 'I need security at the door. PLEASE!'

'It's your own fault for watching those bloody movies,' she snapped, taking a sip from her wine glass. 'I am not going to stand outside the door with a knife while you take a shit.'

Two minutes later she was standing outside the door with a knife while I took a shit.

'Oh for fuck's sake, Rosanna, hurry up.'

'Look, Mum, you can't expect me to rush this. It's an organic process. I think all the drama scared it back in.'

'Oh fuck off,' she said, walking away and leaving me to fend for myself.

The last straw for her, though, came in the middle of the night eleven years later, when I demanded she save me from the Devil, who had taken over my body after I watched *The Exorcist*.

I was eighteen, and living with my wealthy uncle in his very fancy, but very cold, aloof mansion. Everything was open plan and polished floorboards and expensive art that I wasn't allowed to touch, because the oil in my poor-person fingers was poisonous to anything that cost money. One touch from me was enough to make $50,000 worth of paintings immediately crumble into worthless ashes on the floor. And then the expensive floorboards would be damaged so I'd be in double the trouble.

My uncle and his family had gone away on holidays, so I was living in the giant, cold, money mansion by myself for a couple of weeks. And it was on one of those nights, while home alone in a scary house, that I decided to partake in one of my favourite childhood pastimes — pushing myself to a point of fear so torturous and visceral that I would either vomit and/or spend the night under my blanket, completely frozen, looking out of a tiny hole I'd made in the side so I could breathe and see imminent danger.

My uncle had *The Exorcist* on DVD, a magical technology that he'd been watching since it first became a thing. He'd bought a DVD player before you could even really get DVDs anywhere, that's how rich and important he was. Luckily, he lived in a wealthy area with lots of other people who were rich and important enough to buy DVD players without any DVDs to watch on them. So a tiny little store opened at the local shops, next to the place that sold macrobiotic burgers with patties made of grains stuck together with some kind of organic nectar. And this was before Gwyneth started selling that stuff on Goop, along with crystals that you soak in the sun before shoving them up your twat to improve your sex life. And $600 honey from bees that have only been allowed to mate while listening to Beyoncé.

Basically, this wasn't your regular local shops — this was rich people local shops. And that's why it was one of the first places to get a DVD rental store. Not many films had even been released as DVDs at that stage, so the store consisted of a few trays of discs in paper sleeves, which you had to flip through like records. There were maybe a few hundred titles, if that. When you picked what you wanted from the trays, you'd take it to the very snotty man at the counter, and talk for a few minutes about what model DVD player you have, like it was so exclusive to have one you might as well have been comparing private jets. Then you'd go next door and get your macrobiotic food that not even Gwyneth had heard of yet, before heading home to laugh at everybody who still had to watch things on VHS. Savages.

I popped *The Exorcist* in the DVD player at about 7pm. It was dark outside, which made this house a little spooky because, like all rich houses, one entire side was basically made only of windows. It seems like a lovely and very impressive idea, but when you turn the inside lights on at night and can't see anything but an endless dark void through the glass, it's a little off-putting.

It was about halfway through the movie when I started to feel like my heart was beating too quickly. Probably normal, since I was watching a horror film while alone in a dark, scary mansion, but since this particular horror film is about a girl who loses control of her body as Satan takes it over, I started to think that maybe some outside forces were *making* my heart beat too quickly.

In spite of being slightly worried I was slowly losing my soul in a battle with the Devil, I continued to watch the movie. By the time it was over, I was sweating profusely – yet more evidence that I was lost to Satan. The more I thought about it, the more distressed I became, and the quicker my heart would beat. I suddenly became very aware of my body – my breathing seemed deliberate, my heartbeat too fast. I felt itchy all over for no reason. It didn't matter to me that all these physical symptoms were obviously the result of sending myself into a panic via horror film – I had been possessed by the Devil, just like the girl in the movie who stabbed herself in the vagina with a crucifix. The more I panicked, the more my body reacted, and the more my body reacted, the more convinced I became I was possessed, which only increased my panic … I was stuck in an idiotic cycle of self-imposed fear. I knew my uncle didn't have any crucifixes in the house but I put on three pairs of underwear just to be safe.

By about one in the morning I was in total hysterics. I was completely convinced that I was done for. The next step was going to be me yelling sexual obscenities about Jesus and throwing a priest out the window. I could only think of one person to call. The only person on earth with a bubble of murder immunity around them. I needed to call my mother.

'OH FOR FUCK'S *SAKE*, ROSANNA!'

She was not pleased.

'Mum, I swear to god, something is actually happening to me. My breathing is weird and my heart is funny. It's definitely the early stages of possession. I know, because I just watched *The Exorcist*.'

'You're not bloody possessed,' she laughed, not treating the situation with the seriousness I felt it deserved.

'Mum, I think I am. I need to come over. This could be bad.'

I didn't drive. She was obviously too drunk to get into a car, so there was only one solution: a taxi. And she was about forty minutes away. It wasn't going to be cheap, and at eighteen, I didn't have that kind of cash.

I needed to beg her like I used to beg her to let me sleep in her room.

'Please, Mum.'

'No.'

'PLEASE, MUM.'

'Fuck off! No.'

'Please, Mum – I could die!'

'Oh shut the fuck up, Rosanna.'

'Please, Mum.'

'No.'

'Please, Mum.'

'No.'

'Please, Mum.'

'No.'

'Please, Mum.'

'Fucking hell! Alright! Get a bloody cab and I'll pay for it when you get here.'

'Can you call it? I don't like talking on the phone.'

'Oh for FU—' She hung up.

I ended up at Mum's house at about 3am. Straight away, I could tell the Devil was gone. I was in the bubble of murder immunity. My soul would be safe, at least for that night.

I saw Mum putting some blankets on the couch. The couch?

'Oh,' I said, looking longingly into her room. 'Can't I sleep in your bed?'

'JESUS FUCKING CHRIST, ROSANNA.'

I'll never end up with someone like my dad.
(I was in it before I even realised what was happening.)

I couldn't believe I was walking the streets at 10pm, looking for someone who was passed out drunk in the gutter. I also couldn't believe that someone was my boyfriend.

Actually, at that stage, he was my ex-boyfriend. I had been trying to avoid him, but when he called me – so plastered he was barely coherent – and told me he was around the corner, I just told him to walk to my house. I figured I could get him home from there, or at least let him sleep it off on the couch. An hour later, when he still hadn't shown up, I put on my dressing gown and slippers and went looking for him. I found him in less than a minute, about a block away from my house, passed out in the gutter outside someone's front gate.

I immediately had flashbacks to my dad. My dad, the alcoholic, who I'd found like that so many times in my childhood. My dad, who made me sick with anxiety until the day he died. But I was a little girl then – I had no choice. If Dad collapsed while crossing the street or in the bathroom of a restaurant, I couldn't just leave. I was tethered to him, not just by blood, but also by need. He was the only dad I had, and often the only person taking care of me. I had no choice but to stay.

It wasn't like that with Mike, though. When I started dating him, I was twenty-seven. A grown woman with the power to choose what people I would allow into my life. I was the one in charge now, tethered firmly to those I loved by choice. And after a childhood filled with dysfunctional, neglectful and abusive people, I was very strict with my choices.

So why did I choose a man who passed out in the gutter just like my dad?

Mike felt like a safe option when we got together. We had met years earlier, in my late teens, and he'd had an adorable, massive crush on me at the time. It felt lovely to be so admired, but even then, I just had a feeling about him. Something was a bit … off. He seemed sweet and naïve, but every now and then a huge ego would flash through. Each conversation I had with him, I felt like I was talking to a real-life Holden Caulfield. I suppose at the time I sensed an arrogance, or a nastiness, but I was young, so I couldn't quite put my finger on it.

We occasionally kept in touch over Facebook through the years, and one night, sick of being single and missing the warm feeling that comes from knowing someone has a crush on you, I messaged him. We met up later that week, he kissed me in the rain, and we were a couple almost immediately. Even though he lived almost two hours away in Wollongong, we spent almost every day together. I didn't think about why I had rejected him years earlier. I suppose I didn't want to think about that; I just liked not having to be alone.

But the warning signs started pretty early. On our first few dates, he talked a lot about his wasted potential. He'd always wanted to be a writer, or an actor, and he considered himself exceptionally talented at both. But it hadn't worked out for him, and now he was toiling away in a call-centre job that he 'just knew' was beneath him.

'Do you ever feel like you just know, *you just know*, that you're better than other people?' he asked me one night.

I laughed. 'What do you mean?' I was hoping he was joking but scared that he wasn't.

'Well, sometimes I just feel so lucky, because I know that I'm more intelligent, and more talented, than, like, ninety-nine per cent of people. It's not … I mean, I don't mean to sound like a dick, but … it's true. It's just true. Don't you ever feel that? I mean, you're talented, and funny.'

'Um, yeah, I guess,' I said, not wanting to rock the boat in a very new romance. 'I know I'm good at what I do. I'm definitely a talented writer, I guess.'

I didn't quite know how to answer. I was making a living off writing then, but I felt like a fraud every day of my life. I was constantly waiting to be found out, like every piece I wrote was going to be the piece that would finally make somebody say, 'Wow. We really shouldn't be paying Rosie to write anymore. This is just awful. Why did we ever think she had any talent?'

I was living my life waiting for someone to notice I was actually terrible. Mike was living his life waiting for someone to notice he was actually brilliant.

'It's bullshit, it's fucking bullshit, some of the books that get published now. That should be me. I could be this country's Jonathan Franzen.'

Smile. Nod. Agree. I told myself that his confidence was a good thing. It's not like my low self-esteem was a positive; maybe I should try to have more faith in my abilities? Good on him, right?

It wasn't until he started comparing himself to Robin Williams that I started to worry a little about his narcissism. 'It's just so fucking sad,' he said, talking about his death a year earlier. 'It really affected me, the day that he died. I had to call in sick to work, because I just kept thinking how easily that could have been me. I mean, I know how it feels to be so talented, and for that to overwhelm you, you know?'

'Um, yeah.' Wow.

That kind of talk should have turned me right off, but we were right in the middle of the hours and days of talking and learning about each other that everybody does when they think they're falling in love. So, in the grand scheme of things, it was easy to ignore a few comments in which he revealed he considered himself equal to Robin Williams and Jonathan Franzen. Oh, and 'just better' than ninety-nine per cent of all people.

What I really didn't want to admit at the time, although it was glaringly obvious, was that Mike actually had less reason to consider himself brilliant than most people I knew. Despite insisting he was meant for greatness, he never really did anything to achieve it. He also, shockingly, wasn't as talented as he thought. His writing was … not terrible, but not great.

He once decided, since I made money writing online, that it should be easy enough for him to do as well (a subtle dig I ignored). He tried submitting a single piece, once. It was rejected. When I looked over it for him and gave him some gentle suggestions, he couldn't have been more dismissive. 'I'm not going to compromise my style,' he said. 'That's why I'll never work online, I don't want to. It's just about pandering for clicks.' I was an online writer at the time, so that was another subtle dig at my expense. He seemed to really resent my success. I was sometimes approached on the street by people who had read my work, and it always made him quiet and sulky. When I signed my first book deal, I called him immediately, crying with joy, excited to tell him the news. He was the first person I called. There was tense silence on the other end of the phone.

'Yeah. That's great,' he said, not even trying to feign enthusiasm. 'Really great.'

'Is something wrong?' I asked. 'Are you okay?' I knew he hadn't been happy at work – maybe I'd just caught him at a bad time.

'No, no, I'm fine,' he said. 'Just tired.'

I started to tell him more about the deal, but he just didn't seem like he wanted to be on the phone.

'Seriously, are you okay?' I asked. 'You don't seem yourself.'

He took a deep sigh. 'Yeah, look. It's not a big deal. It's just, you know that I want to be a writer, and that my job is fucking depressing, so you just can't … You must know that it's just hard for me to hear this, because I've always wanted to write a book. You must know that.'

'Oh,' I said, a little taken aback.

'Please don't be annoyed, okay? I just thought you would have realised that, that's all.'

'I'm so sorry,' I quickly replied, terrified that I'd screwed up by being so selfish. 'You're right, this would be hard. I'm sorry I didn't think about it …'

The call didn't last much longer. I wasn't sure how to react. Was I annoyed? Or was he right – should I have considered how my good news would affect him? I think he was right. Yes, definitely right. I really should have considered his feelings.

I felt like the excitement had been sucked out of me. I called my best friend, the one person who I knew would react to the happiest moment in my life the exact way that I wanted. And he did.

'OH HOLY FUCKING OPRAH GURL! YOU GONNA BE FAMOUS! YAS YAS YAS YOU DESERVE THIS YOU FUCKING QUEEN! I'M SO EXCITED CONGRATULATIONS I WISH I WAS THERE ARRRRGGHHHHH!'

Tony did not stop screaming for a full minute. I stood, beaming, in the middle of the street.

'Did you tell Mike? Is he flipping out? How are you guys going to celebrate?'

'Um, yeah,' I said. 'I told him, but … It's just really hard for him, you know, because he hates his job and he really wants to write, so … I get it. It must be hard.'

'What's hard?' Tony snapped.

'Just, me doing so well at the moment. It's kind of selfish, to rub it in his face, you know?'

'Uh, fuck that, Ro. Seriously. Fuck that.'

I knew Tony was right, of course. But I didn't want to see it. Or maybe I couldn't. Mike had been belittling my career and writing ability since we first got together, constantly making it clear that he thought what I wrote was mainstream and superficial. He even told me that he thought it was unfair I got a book deal 'just because you had a bad childhood'.

'Well, I'm also a good writer,' I feebly responded. 'They don't give book deals to just anybody.'

'Yeah, but you have to admit that you're lucky you have an interesting story to tell. Why else would you get a memoir deal when you're so young?'

He really thought my success should have been his, and it got to the point where I felt guilty that it wasn't. He told me one night that he had always dated women who were beneath him; that he had always had the upper hand in his relationships because he was the more 'valuable' one in the couple. I was the first woman he'd dated, he said, who had the upper hand over him. He said it made him uncomfortable, but he was working on it. He just needed my understanding.

So I gave it to him. I put all of this down to his insecurity about his failed career ambitions. I kept encouraging him to write. I gave him pointers on how to submit his work. I wanted so badly for him to have the career he wanted, so we could be happy. Because a lot of the time, we were really happy. But he seemed to spend more time complaining about having no opportunities than he did trying to create any. He just seemed determined to be miserable and bitter.

Then there was the drinking. Mike really liked to drink, but he could not hold his booze. Every time we went out, he would fall over, or yell at someone, or cry. And it would happen so suddenly. One second he'd be a bit tipsy along with everyone else; the next, his face would turn bright red, he'd start swaying and slurring his words, and before you knew it, he was screaming at a bodyguard who was asking him to leave.

But I ignored that too. He didn't drink all the time; it was just that when he did, sometimes he didn't know when to stop. We've all been there, right? My alcoholic parents had drunk all day, every day, so I equated drinking problems with constant, consistent excess. I didn't recognise what Mike did as a problem at first. Even though when he drank, I would start to get nervous about how fast he was going, and whether or not he would embarrass me in front of a crowd of people. But it didn't happen all the time, so I figured it was okay. I could ignore it.

Plus he blamed a lot of his drinking on his parents, and his relationship with them really did seem to be deteriorating, so I was trying to be supportive about that as well. He would go on and on about how they were affecting his mental health. How his mother was manipulative and nasty. He would sometimes call me on the verge of tears, having just argued with them about something.

I wanted to help, so when Tony moved to Texas to study for a semester, I told Mike he could take his room. Sure, it was fast (we'd only been together a couple of months), but I just kept trying to think of ways to make him happier. If he left Wollongong and moved in with me for a couple of months, that would fix everything, right?

Mike moving in didn't fix anything. In fact, it made things a lot worse. I hadn't realised how much of his dysfunctional behaviour Mike had been hiding from me. Or maybe, in my desperation to 'keep' him, I'd been ignoring it. But when you live together, those things are impossible to ignore. The red flags turn into neon signs that are flashing right in your face.

His moodiness started to get worse and he struggled to complete regular, adult tasks, like paying his bills, or cleaning or shopping. He didn't seem to have the first idea about how to support himself. When I'd ask him to maybe contribute more around the apartment, he'd sink into a dark mood and say something like, 'See! My mum's fucking right! I *am* useless. I'm sorry I'm fucking useless.'

I started to feel nervous about coming home from work, but also worried that he'd be annoyed if I didn't. It wasn't that he wanted to control where I was; it was just that he seemed to resent anything work-related that made me happy, and I didn't want him to resent me. Like having an article go viral, or making a radio appearance. 'Must be nice to have a job like that,' he'd say, like I was doing well just to make him feel bad.

But I kept going. I kept ignoring. We could make it work, if I just figured out how to make him happy. When he was happy, things were so good. But his bitter moods were so hard to predict. I never knew which Mike I was going to get, and it was making me anxious.

Then, sitting on the couch one night, he suddenly burst into tears. He told me that he'd never been so depressed. That he felt worthless as a person. That he thought about killing himself. That being with me made him feel like a loser. That he hated the fact that life had not given him the things he wanted.

He was hysterical, and it petrified me. I had grown up listening to my parents break down like this. I had grown up feeling the brunt of their erratic moods and instabilities. I had grown up with their drinking and collapsing. I had grown up feeling alone and confused, and in that moment I realised that is what I had been feeling since I started dating Mike. Suddenly I was seeing my parents in front of me. I panicked.

'I can't deal with this,' I said. I told him that I was scared, and I was really sorry, but I didn't think I was the person to help him. Being around him, particularly in this moment, was triggering my PTSD, and that wasn't healthy for either of us. I asked him to spend the night at a friend's house.

The next day, I felt awful. His breakdown had explained everything. He clearly had some kind of mental-health problem that he needed to deal with, and mental health was something I understood. I'd spent years in therapy, trying to overcome the anxiety and PTSD from my childhood. I got it. I was so angry at myself for freaking out the night before – me, of all people, should have empathy for his situation. Managing mental-health problems isn't easy, but it can be done. I knew because I was doing it myself.

I asked him to meet me after work so we could talk about what he'd told me, my reaction, and how we could handle it and get him the help he needed.

I was really surprised when happy, confident, funny Mike turned up. He seemed like a completely different person to the one who had been hysterically crying on the couch the night before.

I started by apologising, telling him I'd been triggered and freaked out. But after having a night to think about it, I was okay. I really wanted to help him. I didn't realise he'd been so depressed that he'd thought about killing himself.

'I'm not depressed,' he said. 'Seriously. I just had a bad day. I promise you I'm fine.'

'Mike, you're not fine. You said you had thoughts about killing yourself. I've been there. I know how awful that feels.'

'I don't know why I said that,' he casually replied. 'Honestly, I feel fine now. I'm really sorry that it scared you.'

This wasn't the conversation I had expected.

'Mike, you may feel better today, but you're not fine. You were hysterical last night. You said you'd had suicidal thoughts. I understand that the feeling may have gone, but something caused you to break down like that. And looking back over the last couple of months, I can see a pattern there. Your moods are so erratic. I just didn't realise how bad it was.'

'It's not bad, though!' he insisted.

'I think you need help,' I said, ignoring him. 'You need to see a psychiatrist. Maybe even go on medication if they think that's what you need.'

'I'm not going on medication,' he snapped.

'Look, you might not have to. But you definitely need help, Mike. After last night … You're not well. You may feel better today, but you're not well. But it's nothing to be ashamed of! Getting help is so doable. We can work on this together.'

'There's nothing to work on, Rosie. I'm fine. I just had a bad day.'

He was flat-out refusing to acknowledge that anything was wrong, which really scared me. I understood mental illness, and I had empathy for what he was going through. But he needed to be willing to take steps to get better. He wasn't.

So, I told him we had to end it. I didn't want to, but I knew I couldn't be with someone who refused to acknowledge their mental health as an issue. I couldn't relive my past.

I held my head high, walked out of the bar and never saw him again.

Ha.

When I walked into my empty apartment, I immediately regretted my healthy decision. I wanted to go back to ignoring everything. I didn't care; I just didn't want to be alone. Any relationship was better than being alone. I called him, in tears.

'Mike, I'm so sorry! I shouldn't have ended it! I'm an idiot! I don't care, just come home!'

I thought he'd be relieved and come back straight away. Not exactly.

'I'm sorry, Rosie,' he said. 'You really let me down. I needed you to comfort me last night and you asked me to leave. And tonight you break up with me? I never thought you would be like this. You were right. I can't be with you. It's over.'

What?

The next half an hour was a very sorry display that anybody who has ever been dumped will understand. I cried. I pleaded. I reasoned. Nothing worked. I took responsibility for everything that had gone wrong and apologised. I had been so selfish. I could do better. I had freaked out momentarily but I would never let him down again.

I was begging him not to leave me. Finally, he had that upper hand he had been so uncomfortable without. I didn't realise that this was exactly how he had wanted this to turn out.

'Look, maybe I can come over tomorrow, it depends how I'm feeling,' he said. 'But I can't promise anything. I just feel so betrayed.'

'I'm sorry, I'm so sorry,' I cried into the phone. I was desperate not to be alone, and my survival instincts had kicked in. I was completely blind to his faults. Exactly like it had been with my parents when I was younger. Having them around, no matter how bad they were, was better than not having them at all.

He spent the next few weeks coming to my house, alluding to a possible reconciliation, having sex with me, then leaving. He had complete control. He would get back together with me for a day, then change his mind in the morning. He told me he loved me and wanted to be with me, the night before a friend's wedding, then texted me when he knew I'd be at the reception and broke it off again. At one point, he told me he couldn't be with me, while he was actually *inside* me. Always because he just couldn't get over my 'betrayal'. He needed someone he could rely on, someone who hadn't been so selfish.

I was broken. Exhausted. Anxious. I could hardly work. I couldn't sleep. I was barely eating. I just didn't trust my instincts anymore. I felt like I was in a dark room, and only he controlled when I could see light. But when the light shone though, nothing made sense. I had lost myself.

Funnily enough, during this period of total emotional annihilation, he stopped being resentful about my career. I suppose there was nothing to resent anymore, since he no longer considered me the more 'valuable' person in our relationship. Keeping me hanging had put him back on top, just the way he had once told me he liked it.

But, in the end, it wasn't the emotional abuse that snapped me out of it; I was too broken for that. It was his drinking. It wasn't until I looked at him, crying on the step outside my house, lying face down on the concrete like a toddler and refusing to get up, that I finally realised I had been dating someone exactly like my dad. The mental-health stuff, the moodiness, the uneasiness in the pit of my stomach – that had all been familiar to me. Those had all been warnings. But something about seeing Mike on the ground, drunkenly raving … Something about how pathetic that was finally made my brain wake up. It finally clicked: Rosie, you have ended up with the person you said you would never end up with. This is not the man for you. I kicked my way out of the dark room and found my own damn light.

Still face down on the concrete, he was talking about wanting to kill himself again, so I called a close friend of his to come and pick him up. It took this guy twenty minutes just to coax him off my front step. Mike was ranting incoherently, falling as he tried to walk. And I just wanted him to be as far away from me as possible. It was like a blindfold had been pulled off my face. I couldn't believe that I hadn't seen it before.

Then he left, and I never saw him again.

Ha.

I saw him one more time. When I went looking for him at 10pm and found him passed out in the gutter. I really hadn't wanted to see him again, but he did not sound good on the phone. My childhood instincts kicked in: always go and find the drunk person.

'Rosie! You came! You came and found me!' he slurred, when I woke him up. 'You're my hero. I love you, Rosie. You know I love you.'

I took him back to my place, and he started talking about wanting to get back together. He had become so used to me begging him, and gratefully accepting any emotional scrap he threw at me, that he did not like it when I said no. First he picked a fight with me. He got really nasty. He told me I was a fraud, because my first book was going to be about my difficult childhood, but he knew that my uncle had sent me to a private boarding school when I turned fifteen.

'How fucking hard could it have been? You went to a better school than me! You're so full of shit, Rosie.'

I knew that he was drunk. I knew that he was desperate. I knew he was trying to get a reaction out of me. He got one.

'Well you know what?' I screamed. 'You are a TERRIBLE FUCKING WRITER. You haven't been unlucky – people just don't want to read your work BECAUSE IT'S SHIT.'

He stared at me. I stared right back at him. Then he burst into tears, grabbed a massive knife from the kitchen and locked himself in the bathroom. He was wailing and screaming, threatening to kill himself, so I called Triple Zero.

He must have heard me on the phone, because the bathroom went quiet. Then I heard the door unlock, and he came running towards me. He pushed me up against the inside of the front door and held the knife up to my face. 'I will fucking use this, Rosie. I'll use it.'

'Is that him?' the woman on the line asked.

'Um, yes,' I stammered. 'He, ah, he has a knife. I mean, he said he wants to use it. I think he just means on himself, though. Um, let me call you back.' I hung up the phone.

'Rosie, let me out of this fucking house. Just let me go so I can throw myself in front of a car.'

I didn't know what to do. I didn't want to let him out if he was going to hurt himself. He'd also just held a knife up to my face. I didn't think he meant he wanted to use it on me. I did think he meant himself. He was drunk, and not making a lot of sense. My brain had a million thoughts and no thoughts at the same time. Like it had short-circuited. I opened the door and let him out. Then my phone rang.

'Rosie, is that you?' It was the same operator.

'Yes,' I said. 'I'm sorry I hung up, I just … Um …'

'You can't hang up again, Rosie. Where is he now? Is he in the house?'

'No, I let him out of the house. He said he wanted to leave.'

'Because you mentioned he had a weapon, Rosie, I had to send police officers. Stay on the line with me until they get there.'

Police? What? Had I actually turned into the girl who needs to have police remove a guy from her house? After everything

I had been through as a child, after everything I had seen, how could I be so stupid? How could I have ended up in the kind of stressful domestic situation I had promised myself I'd never return to? How could I have ended up with someone like my dad?

The police were there within about two minutes. Mike hadn't gone and thrown himself in front of a car. He was hiding down the side of my apartment building, crying. The police grabbed him and slammed him up against a wall. I immediately felt guilty – they were looking for a 'weapon' because I had told the woman on the phone he had one. But I didn't mean for him to sound threatening. I just wanted … I don't know what I wanted. I just didn't want it to be my problem anymore.

I assured the police that he hadn't threatened to harm me, just himself. I told them that he was incredibly mentally unwell, had been for some time, and I thought he needed to be hospitalised. They called for an ambulance.

He was taken to sit in the back of it as soon as it parked out the front. I asked them to wait, since I had called Mike's good friend again, and he was on his way. I waited in my living room, just desperate for the whole thing to be over. I got a call on my phone from a private number. I thought it might be Mike's friend so I answered. It was Mike. He was calling from the back of the ambulance parked out the front.

'I really don't want to be talking to you,' I said, annoyed that I'd been tricked into picking up a call from him.

'They're taking me away,' he said.

'You'll just go to the ER, then they'll let you out,' I replied. 'But Mike, you have to be honest with them about how you've been feeling. You really need help.'

'I'm fine, Rosie.'

And that was it. The police asked me if I wanted to press charges, but I said no. I just really wanted him to get help. He was narcissistic, emotionally abusive, and not even close to being as talented as Robin Williams. But I just really wanted him to get help.

I hope he got it.

The car trip to Griffith the day before Tony's funeral was actually kind of ... fun. My older sister Rhiannon, my younger sister Tayla, and Rhiannon's two kids, Allira and Mohammed, were crammed into the car. Mohammed was only three, so I sat in the back next to him and let him watch movies on my laptop. I thought about working on the eulogy, but knew there was no point. Whatever I had written in that thing, it had taken a miracle for my brain to get it on the page. There was no way I was going to manage anything else.

We stopped at Maccas on the way, and laughed and told stories the way people are forced to only when stuck in a car together for eight hours. Mo and I watched *The Little Mermaid*, and I tried not to think about the fact I would be seeing Tony's body before I went to bed that night.

I'd never seen a dead body before. When my dad died, when I was eight, I had tentatively asked my mum if we could see him in the coffin.

She seemed taken aback. 'Is that something you want to do?' she asked me. I felt like I had asked something wrong. She seemed ... disturbed.

'No,' I quickly blurted out. 'No, I don't want to.'

Years later, when my grandma died, the whole family was taken to a small waiting room before the funeral service. There was a door off to the side, which someone mentioned was the entrance to 'the viewing room'. I knew what that meant. I did not want to go into that room. I was the only one who felt that way. At thirteen, I may have been young, but even six-year-old Tayla was brave enough to go in. The entire family went in together, so I just sat there alone, waiting for them to finish 'viewing' on the other side of the door.

Tayla came bursting out of the room approximately eight seconds after she had gone in. The look on her face made me realise I'd made the right decision. She looked confused, bewildered and a little terrified. She handled it so well, though. After hurriedly coming out of that room, she just quietly walked over to the chair next to me, sat on it, and didn't say a word as we waited for everyone else to come out. She must have been busting to talk about what she'd just seen, but even at six years old, she sensed this was a moment for respectful silence.

I've always been glad that I didn't go into that room, because I didn't want that to be the last memory I had of my grandma. I knew if I saw her that way, I'd never be able to think of her without thinking of her inside that viewing room. And the last memory I had of her was pretty great. My grandma was a very stylish lady – she was getting her hair coloured and washed and blow-dried until the day she died. I went to stay with her and Grandpa for a couple of days once, and she had to take me to the salon to get my hair washed, because she actually just didn't keep shampoo anywhere in the house. I don't think she'd washed her own hair since the 1960s.

She was dressed immaculately every day, and she loved buying clothes for my sisters and me. She was a little judgemental, but always delivered with the right amount of posh sass so that it was charming. Towards the end, when it looked like she only had days left, my mum took us to the hospital to see her. I'll never forget the last thing she said to me. She gestured for me to lean in close to her, and dramatically pulled off her oxygen mask, like she had something very important to say. I bent down as close to her face as I could get, ready to take in whatever departing life wisdom she had to offer me.

'That's a nice top,' she said. 'Since when are you so stylish?'

'You bought this for me, Nanna!' I replied.

'Well,' she said, putting her mask back on. 'That explains it.'

I knew I didn't *want* to see Tony's body, but something in me felt like I had to. Because he was overseas when he died, I almost felt like I would never believe it unless I saw the ultimate proof. Like I'd always, somewhere in the back of my mind, hope or imagine that he was still travelling somewhere. That it was all a mistake and he'd make his way home. I couldn't go on living like that. I needed to see him.

As we got closer and closer to Griffith, I started wondering when and if I was going to cry, which I still hadn't really done since Tony had died. I had shed some tears, but not even come close to breaking down yet. And I wanted to. I could still see all my pain just sitting there in the glass jar, and I wanted it out. I needed the lid to come completely off, before the fear of it coming off drove me crazy.

Would it happen when I saw Tony's parents? His sister? His nieces and nephews? Maybe when I saw Tony? Or tomorrow at the funeral. Or when I was trying to read his eulogy with Assunta. I wish I knew when the explosion was going to come.

Tony's Italian family are very proud Catholics, which meant death was handled in a certain way that my sisters and I had never experienced. Every funeral I'd ever been to was a small service, followed by a sensible reception, ending with everybody going home to their own houses.

That is not how things are done in the incredibly loving and supportive Griffith Italian community. First of all, the entire family – that's extended family – converged on Tony's parents' house, a little place on a farm on the outskirts of Griffith, where Tony spent his childhood.

The extended family formed a support circle around Tony's parents. They took turns sleeping there, they cooked, they cleaned, they built a marquee next to the house so everybody could sit down to meals together. The family split into two rooms in the house – the men in one room grieving with Pat, Tony's dad, and the women in another room, grieving with Maria, Tony's mother. They all wore black, and in the centre of the room was a shrine to Tony, covered in photos and rosaries and mementos. Sarina, Tony's sister, told me that after the funeral, this arrangement would stay in place for at least a month. Tony's immediate family needed to grieve, so his extended family would take care of everything else. The support circle was breathtakingly beautiful in its love.

My heart started to beat faster as my sisters and I pulled up to Tony's house. His best friend Assunta met at us the end of the dirt driveway. We hugged and laughed and commented on how neither of us could believe the whole thing. She seemed jittery, agitated. Looked like I wasn't the only one keeping a lid on their glass jar.

I went inside. In the living room, all the women in Tony's family were sitting around his shrine, holding hands, with his mother Maria in the centre. She looked up. We locked eyes. I've never seen so much sorrow on a person's face. She jumped up out of her chair and threw her arms around me. We stayed locked in that position for a long time. I wish I could remember what I said. What she said. But I just remember her embrace: equal parts generous in its comfort and heartbreaking in its anguish. I didn't want to let go. My sisters and I talked with the rest of the family, making awkward introductions with people we'd never met – like 'Hi! It's so lovely to meet you! Except, you know, Tony's dead and nobody's heart will ever get over the pain and emptiness we're feeling right now. But I've heard so much about you!'

It went by in such a blur, by the time we left I didn't even realise that I still hadn't cried.

Assunta came back to our hotel with us, because she and I were going to drive over to the viewing together. We went up to our room, hung out with the kids, joked about how bizarre everything was. She and I seemed to be handling things the same way: block all feelings. Make jokes. Get jobs done. Concentrate on details. We talked about the eulogy I had sent through, which she and Sarina had loved, although at that point I couldn't remember what the hell was in it.

Then it was time to go. Time to go and see the body. Time to go and see Tony's dead body. How the fuck was this actually happening?

We kept talking in the car on the way over to the funeral home. I asked her what to expect, and explained what it had been like with my grandma.

'Wow,' she said, laughing. 'This is nothing like that.'

She explained that Tony would be at the front of a large room filled with chairs. It was tradition for everybody to come and see the body. People line up, she said, and once they've had their turn walking past the coffin, they go and sit in the chairs and pray. The line is usually long, and would definitely be really long for Tony.

The only clear memory I have of the next half an hour is Tony's face. The rest is ... fuzzy with insignificance. We arrived at the funeral home. We parked the car, which just seemed like a bizarrely normal thing to do. The line was already out the door. We joined it, along with Tony's closest cousins. We chatted as we inched forward, waiting for our turn. We got inside the room. I saw the coffin. I saw the outline of Tony's face. I spun around and faced the other direction.

'I saw him,' I said to Assunta. 'I shouldn't have looked. I saw him.'

I could feel my lid coming off. I'd never had so much adrenalin coursing through every inch of my body. Every pore on my skin was tingling. Every hair standing on end. The line inched forward.

Assunta put her arm around me. I could tell from her face that her lid was close to coming off too. The line inched forward.

Assunta told me she had a bracelet that she wanted to put in the coffin with Tony. I panicked that I hadn't thought to bring anything. The line inched forward.

I could see Tony's parents, sitting in the front row, right beside his coffin. I caught another glimpse of him. My heart jumped. My mouth went dry. The line inched forward.

Not now, I kept thinking. Not. Now. Everything couldn't come exploding out of me now. Not in that room. Not while surrounded by the people who had lost the dearest member of their family. I would not want to obligate them to comfort me at a time like this. This was about them. Hold it the fuck together, Rosie.

Assunta and I finally reached the front of the line. We stepped forward, and I looked down at my soulmate, lying in his coffin.

Tony was dressed in a chequered suit, his hands folded neatly on his chest, holding a rosary. But it didn't look like Tony. It just looked like a version of him. Like a wax figure. I reached down to touch his hand. The hand that had held mine since the day he met me. The hand that had kept me safe and made me brave. The hand that I wasn't ready to let go.

It was hard. Like plastic. My fingers recoiled and I took a sharp breath in. I had expected the man lying in this coffin to just be Tony, but asleep. I thought he'd look like the man I woke up next to after we fell asleep watching movies, usually a pizza box between us. This wasn't sleeping Tony. This was something else. That wasn't the hand I remembered.

I thought maybe his face would be different, so I reached over and stroked his cheek. Again, my hand jerked back. His face felt the same as his hand. Cold. Hard. Like a doll. Just like a plastic doll.

My brain was reeling. Every nerve ending in my body was on fire. This wasn't my best friend. This wasn't my soulmate. This was a plastic doll in a chequered suit.

The lid was finally about to burst off my glass jar. I wasn't sure I could do anything to stop it. But before it could happen, Assunta reached into the coffin and placed the bracelet next to Tony's hands. It immediately slipped off and down the side of his body, and we both looked at each other, eyes wide, as it rattled against the side of the coffin as it slid all … the way down … to the bottom. It was a quiet room, and that bracelet slipping off Tony's lap and into the coffin abyss might as well have been as loud as a marching band. I pursed my lips together, trying not to laugh. So did Assunta. Then, before I realised we had been moved on, we were walking towards the back of the room. Assunta asked if I wanted to stay and pray. 'No,' I said. 'I think I really need to leave.'

I turned around, took one last look at Tony lying there in his chequered suit, and I walked out the door.

'Oh my god, the bracelet!' Assunta said, once we were in the car. We laughed and laughed, and talked about how much Tony would love that her gift to him was probably now wedged under his bum for eternity. I didn't tell her that I was grateful it had happened when it did, because I was certain that just a moment before, my legs had been about to give out.

Everybody was going back to Tony's house for dinner after the viewing, but I asked Assunta just to drop me back at the hotel with my sisters. I felt like I hadn't taken a breath since the moment I had looked at Tony's face, and laughing about the bracelet was only a temporary fix. Something big was coming. I could feel it.

Jacob, who had driven up from Melbourne, arrived while I was at the viewing, so we all decided to go to dinner together. We found some Italian restaurant down the road, and set ourselves up at a table big enough to fit other friends from drama school who were on their way. I still felt like I hadn't taken a breath. I still felt tingles all over my body. I started just nodding or shaking my head when Jacob or one of my sisters tried to talk to me, like just pushing words out was going to be the thing that would make me explode. I sat at the table, listening to Rhiannon try and order something that Mohammed would eat, watching the families around me laugh and chat and enjoy each other's company. I sat while Jacob tried to explain to an Italian waiter that he didn't eat gluten or dairy or sugar or meat or onion or garlic. I sat there, in that crowded restaurant, and all I could see was a plastic doll in a chequered suit.

'I need to go to the bathroom,' I said, jumping out of my chair.

'Are you okay, Rosie?' Jacob asked.

'I just need the bathroom,' I snapped. 'I'm just ... The bathroom!'

I practically sprinted away from the table. I couldn't breathe. I needed air.

The bathroom was three levels up, in the dark, closed mini-mall that the restaurant was connected to. I stood on each escalator, trembling, knowing that whatever had been bubbling under the surface was coming out now. Right now. The bathroom was locked, so I walked through the dark mall and found a bench outside an empty store. I sat down, clung to the wooden slats beneath my fingers and stared at the ground.

It was here.

I let out a guttural scream like nothing I had ever heard before. I didn't know I could make a sound like that. I howled in anguish and struggled to breathe through my heaving sobs. Every spark of energy that had built up in my body since the day I found out Tony had died was now exploding out of me all at once. The lid had been blown off the glass jar, and the pain it released was hitting me like a freight train.

I screamed, I cried, I howled, I wailed. I sat alone on that bench in the dark, finally realising that Tony was gone. If I reached out my hand, he wouldn't be there to hold it. Tony was dead. And I was alone.

Once I managed to get control over my body again, I started to make my way back down to the restaurant. The visceral and the emotional had finally clashed, and now I was supposed to go eat some garlic bread. I must have been gone a while, because by the time I got back to our table, the meals had arrived along with our other friends from drama school. I saw how I must have looked in their horrified expressions. Everyone at the table knew I must have just finally broken down. No one said a word about it. We had a nice dinner and went back to the hotel, ready for the funeral in the morning.

Rhiannon woke me up by asking what I wanted for breakfast. 'Just a toasted sandwich or something,' I replied, assuming she was going to one of the cafés downstairs. When she came back with McDonald's for everyone else and a toasted sandwich for me, I lost it.

'What the fuck? Why didn't I get McDonald's?'

'Because you said you wanted a toasted sandwich!'

'But that's only because I didn't know McDonald's was an option! Have you ever known anyone to pick a shitty toasted sandwich over a fucking hashbrown? WHY WOULDN'T I WANT A HASHBROWN? And why wouldn't you specify that you're going to McDonald's when you ask me what I want for breakfast? Why would you ask me what I want without using the word "McDonald's" at any point? I'm not a fucking mind reader. How the fuck was I supposed to know that you were going to McDonald's, and that I had the entire McDonald's breakfast menu to choose from, which meant I never would have chosen a SHITTY FUCKING TOASTED SANDWICH?'

I may not have been in the healthiest of emotional states.

I also yelled at Tayla for how long she was taking in the shower and at Rhiannon again for not letting me use the GHD at the exact moment I required it. I was slightly on edge.

There had to have been over a thousand people at the funeral. Tony is the only person I know whose funeral needed bouncers. The church was standing room only, and a large hall next door with a live video stream was also full. Bouncers and a live video stream. Tony would have loved it. People who didn't fit into the church or hall spilled out onto the front steps, then the footpath, then the road.

I took my seat next to Assunta, a few rows from the front. Jacob somehow hustled himself and my sisters into the back of the church. Just like the viewing, it went by in a blur for me. I do remember that it was a beautiful, traditional, Catholic service. Flowers from all over the world filled the church. Tony's presence reached far and wide.

Assunta had been worried that she'd break down while reading her half of the eulogy, so I stood with my arm around her, ready to take over. But she nailed every word. As I stepped to the lectern to deliver my half, I saw Jacob, always a head above everybody else in the room, standing at the back of the church. We locked eyes. He smiled. I was so glad he had hustled his way in.

After the service, we made our way over to the cemetery. Hundreds of people gathered around Tony's sky blue coffin, before three doves were released into the air. One dove stayed firmly on the ground, and kind of waddled slowly around in a circle. We called that the 'Can't Be Fucked Dove'. That would have been Tony's favourite dove.

Everybody was handed a colourful balloon, and we all released them into the air simultaneously. I've never seen hundreds of balloons float into the sky like that before. They flock together like birds, moving wildly, but as a unit. (I'd probably never seen it because it's illegal. Later, when speaking to Tony's brother-in-law Bruno, he told me that the guy at the balloon shop had said that no more than twenty balloons can be released at any one time. 'Mate,' Bruno said, looking him dead in the eye and clearly not messing around, 'we're going to need three hundred.')

As Tony's coffin was lowered into the ground, his family gathered around the grave. I stepped back, but his nonna pulled me in close to her, and whispered to me, 'He was your family, too.'

That his family found it within themselves to be so generous to me in their time of gut-wrenching sorrow ... Well, that's probably why Tony was so brilliant. He came from the best.

Later that day, there was a wake at Tony's house. Grief filled the air, but Tony had been so spectacular, so full of life, that the kind of people he connected with were the kind who wanted to celebrate him just as much as mourn him. His drama-school friends mixed with his Italian aunties. His high-school friends swapped stories with his Melbourne friends. His cousins laughed with my sisters. My nephew played with his nephew (and they hated each other, which Tony would have found hilarious).

In the evening, we all sat at long tables in the marquee set up next to the house and ate pasta together, which had been lovingly prepared by the brilliant people in his family.

The night ended with all of us linking arms in a giant circle as we sang Tony's favourite song, one all of us had heard him belt out at the top of his lungs at one time or another: 'Part of Your World' from *The Little Mermaid*. Tony's mum sent my sisters and me back to the hotel with about three weeks' worth of food, just in case we needed it before the morning. The best of the best.

The next day, I was driving back to my apartment in Melbourne, so I needed to say goodbye to my sisters and go with Jacob. We stopped off at Tony's parents' place to say goodbye, then we were on our way. As we pulled out of Griffith there was a storm in the distance, and the sky in front of us filled with countless rainbows, spreading across the vineyards as far as we could see. Neither of us acknowledged it. In fact, we didn't talk the entire trip home. We just sang along to five different musical soundtracks, as well as the best of Christina Aguilera. Maybe it was because we were too emotionally exhausted, but that was all we needed to debrief.

As we pulled into Melbourne, I tried to take stock of the last couple of weeks. Okay, I thought. You had it. You had your breakdown. You cried on that bench and saw his coffin go into the ground. Now you have closure: you smashed the glass jar and let the pain out. Everything is going to be better after today.

The IV hooked up to my arm in the emergency room would beg to differ.

It's Jaaaaack's Suuuuuubwaaaaaay Tuuuuuuuuush.

I've never hoped that my mum would die.
(I have. Recently.)

A lot of people asked me about Rosie's Chicken Soup after I first wrote about it. First, they wanted to know if my mum really was 'that bad', if I really had been forced to start making it so young. Yes. I started making Rosie's Chicken Soup when I was about eight years old. It came about by necessity really, when my mother, an alcoholic with a pretty severe mood disorder, started to treat being at home as … an *optional* part of her routine.

My father had died not long before, sitting in his favourite chair with an empty bottle of pills beside him, and although they had been separated for years, his death broke something in my mum. Any hope I had that she would 'fix herself' and take care of me – that she would fix herself and be one of the mums who coaches netball and picks me up on time and doesn't drink lots of wine from a box in the fridge – disappeared into the ground with my dad. At eight years old, I knew better than to hope. Hope just meant anxious disappointment. You might get a warm, fuzzy feeling when your mum tucks you in at night, but that doesn't mean she won't be gone in the morning, leaving you and your older sister to decide who'll go to school and who'll stay home and look after the baby.

The times at home alone were unsettling, and often a little scary, but mostly they were just exasperating. A lot of work goes into pretending you have a stable parenting situation. There are teachers to fool and neighbours to keep in the dark. But there are also logistical things that need to be handled, things that aren't often covered in modern Dickensian tales of childhood woe and neglect, where sad children with dirty faces stare at you in black and white charity ads on TV. Uniforms need to be cleaned. Lunches need to be packed. Nappies need to be purchased. And, of course, meals need to be cooked.

That is how Rosie's Chicken Soup came to be.

The other thing people always ask me about Rosie's Chicken Soup is what the recipe is, which I find a little perplexing, because I assumed I had made that pretty clear: boil water in saucepan. Put pasta into saucepan (any pasta will do; I like spirals, but sometimes I go with spaghetti). Put powdered chicken stock into water. Wait for pasta to go soft. Pour entire contents into bowl. Eat.

That is the recipe, people. That's it. I wasn't kidding when I said it was an acquired taste. Also, I was eight, so give me a break.

I'm thirty now, and Rosie's Chicken Soup has been my go-to meal since those childhood nights spent alone. In every one of the countless homes and towns I lived in. In every foster home or family member I was placed with. At every one of the twenty-plus schools I ended up attending. Through drama school and university, serious partners and my first job as a writer, Rosie's Chicken Soup was there. And even now, as a grown woman (arguably), living the professional life I always dreamed about, certainly able to afford to eat better than powdered chicken stock with water and pasta, I still come back to Rosie's Chicken Soup. It's my comfort food. It reminds me of my childhood. It's my version of homely nostalgia.

Then my mum saw me make it, and she was horrified.

'What on EARTH is that?' she screamed recently, looking into the gluggy, chicken flavoured abyss that was my saucepan on the stove.

My mum is sober. She is also judging my most prized (and only) culinary offering. But she is *sober*. And she has been since July 2016, which is by far the longest period in my life I've ever known her this way.

After years of rehabs and programs and promises and failures, my sisters and I had mostly given up. I was permanently removed from her care when I was fourteen, and I've had rules in place since then: don't answer her calls after 5pm. Only visit her during the day. Don't get your hopes up.

In early 2016, those rules were easy to follow. It was fairly certain she was going to die; she had been told if she kept going like she had been, it was inevitable. She hadn't left the house for more than a few hours in years. As far as I could tell, her days involved waking up, drinking, sleeping a little, drinking, sleeping a little more, drinking, repeat. At what I was sure was the end, she couldn't keep any food down. Her stomach and ankles were grotesquely swollen, while the rest of her body was freakishly thin. Her skin was grey and her eyes were … lifeless. I found her in bed one day, barely able to move, vomit on the floor next to her and urine through her sheets. She couldn't walk on her own, so I showered her and helped her dress. To me, that day was it: my mother was gone. The sooner she actually died, I thought, the better. She would at least be at peace. As long as she was half-alive like this, we were all in purgatory. And I was done waiting.

And then, maybe because she was closer to the end than she'd ever been before, or maybe there was just a cliff-hanger on TV that she really wanted to see through, she decided to turn around and come back.

Just like that, my mum came back.

She was hospitalised for six weeks, detoxing, recovering and slowly coming out of the fog she's been in since I was a child. Then one day, like something out of every dream I've been having since I was five years old, she stepped out of that hospital in July last year and hasn't had a drink since.

She moved in with me a few months later, and since then, I've been watching her rediscover the world. She's gone from needing me to walk with her to the local shops, to catching the bus into the city by herself because she saw online that 'Country Road is having a sale'. She has a Fitbit and an iPad. She loves podcasts and is obsessed with *My Kitchen Rules*.

And it's all just been so … *bizarre* to me. I'm getting to know a person who I remember only fuzzy snippets of. I'm seeing where I get my humour, silliness and charisma. I want to kill her when I have to explain how to forward an email, eleven times, before she gets it. It infuriates me when she tells me just as I'm leaving the house that what I'm wearing doesn't suit me. And I will actually lose it next time she comes and opens my curtains if I'm still asleep at 10am.

At thirty years old, I have finally found myself one half of a proper mother–daughter relationship.

And yet. And yet. There's that 'hope' thing eating away at me. I want to let this newfound reality envelop me like the warm hugs I always craved. I want to lose myself in it so, so much. But I have been training myself since I was eight years old not to hope. Hope is dangerous. Hope just leads to anxious disappointment. A warm hug will always turn cold.

Won't it?

When I explained to my mum that what she was seeing on the stovetop was Rosie's Chicken Soup, she was horrified. Not because of the history that had gone into me teaching myself to make it, but because the actual soup itself does look kind of horrifying. She immediately decided to show me how it should be done. That night, while I watched TV in my room, I could hear her tinkering away in the kitchen, chopping vegetables, putting (to my complete shock) an entire chicken into a large pot that I didn't even know I owned. She spent hours cooking it, seasoning it, letting it simmer, getting it just right. Then she called me to the kitchen.

'Rosie! Dinner!'

What a strange sound.

She scooped it proudly, lovingly, into bowls, with a ladle, and we sat together, at the dining table, eating chicken soup, the way it's meant to be made.

I liked it. I really, really liked it.

I know hope is dangerous. I know the eight-year-old inside of me is telling me that this won't last, that hope only leads to anxious disappointment.

But I think I'm going to let my mum keep making me proper chicken soup for a while. Maybe this time, the warm hug won't turn cold.

When I'm home alone, I always look sexy and never do anything weird.
(*laughs uproariously*)

There once was a time, when I got out of the shower, that I realised I had allowed the hair on my legs to grow so long that my towel alone was not enough to dry them. That's how I found myself, at 11.45pm, standing completely naked in the middle of my bedroom while I bent over and blow-dried my legs.

Also at that moment, I suddenly found myself eyeing off my dripping, glistening pubes, and obviously I decided the same useful system should apply to them. And let me tell you: figuring out that I could use the hairdryer on places other than my head was a revelation. I've not had to do the butt-floss manoeuvre with my towel a single time since. It streamlined my entire shower routine.

I'm single, I'm thirty, I live alone, and I do some weird shit. Squatting over the carpet while I blast hot air onto my snatch is just the tip of a very suspect iceberg.

And I refuse to believe that I'm the only woman who behaves in a breathtakingly disgusting manner when she is home alone. I know I'm *meant* to believe that I'm the only one; everybody is. When Carrie Bradshaw from *Sex and the City* was home alone, the most 'shameful' thing she did was read *Vogue* at her kitchen bench while eating crackers. And most single women in movies behave as if their apartment is located inside a horny man's brain – she'll mop the house while wearing cute underwear and a cropped T-shirt, not realising there's an adorable little blob of bubbles perfectly positioned on her nose as she sings along to a Taylor Swift song, dancing in a way that is just so accidentally sexy.

The closest I've come to either of those scenarios is sitting on the couch in my undies while I watch TV, drinking wine straight from the bottle and wiping my potato-gem fingers on my boob. Carrie Bradshaw's shameful secret behaviour sounds so classy I'd probably film myself doing it and put it on my dating profile.

If I were sitting at that table with Carrie and the girls, or at a table with any group of women on any TV show, I'd drop so many disgusting truth bombs that we'd immediately be taken off air by the prudish male executives who are the experts on how 'real women' look and act.

'Ladies,' I'd say, staring at three women who are all played by Sarah Jessica Parker, 'you know when you're home alone, and you fart on your hand and smell it, just because you're curious?'

'You fart?' one of the Sarahs would reply.

'Ah, yeah,' I'd say, leaning in to take a sip of my cosmo. 'Actually, don't tell anyone this, but I also *shit*.'

They'd recoil in horror, but would secretly be relieved that they're not the only ones. At least about the shitting part. The farting on the hand thing, I'm not so sure. I don't know where the urge to do that comes from. I don't do it all the time (I've got class), but occasionally, when curiosity overwhelms me, I stick my hand in the line of fire and smell the worst of what my body can produce. I suppose there's a sense of narcissism to it that I probably shouldn't delve too deeply into. I'm not sure what that says about me. But I do like that it says I'm at a point in my life where I'm independent, powerful, self-sufficient, and can afford my own apartment in which I can fart on my own damn hand and smell it in peace.

In my next attempt to corrupt the perfect, cocktail-sipping Sarahs on the TV show in my dreams, I'd tell them about the underground universe of bad-skin delights that is pimple-popping videos. I have manipulated the actual space-time continuum while looking at pimple-popping videos. Like people who insist they've been abducted by aliens because they can't remember three hours out of their day. Or like anyone who's ever run into Kmart to get batteries and wanders out six hours later, in a daze, with an entire new living room set and a bright orange Teflon spatula.

Pimple-popping videos are the Kmart of the internet. I first came across one online, probably after seeing a Buzzfeed headline that screamed something like, 'Watch a woman squeeze three years' worth of pus out of this man's neck!' which is exactly the kind of subtle thing that would make me say, 'YES THANKS,' and immediately click.

From that first viewing, I followed a video trail that I'm yet to find the end of.

'Blackheads on man's back.'

'Popping whiteheads and blackheads close up.'

'HUGE volcanic pimple eruption!'

'You won't believe how much comes out of this guy's ear pimple.'

'Peaceful and satisfying removal: blackheads on nose.'

The videos are varied in their approach to the artform, but I love them all. I'm just not sure anything brings me as much pleasure as watching a blackhead turn into an empty pore. It probably started when I was a child, running away from my mother screaming when she stared at my nose and said something like, 'Rosie! That's a really big one! PLEASE let me get it!' After having let her 'get it' once before, I knew the pain that came with blackhead squeezing and refused to allow her to hack away at my face again. Until we negotiated a price.

My mother was so desperate to squeeze my blackheads that she was willing to pay me five dollars for every single one she pressed her fingernails against. She was a woman possessed, and I never quite understood it until I saw the blackheads on my first boyfriend. Lying in bed together, romantically intertwined, I'd stare loving into his back until I became fixated on a single blackhead. Then another. Then another. All I'd have to do is apply the tiniest amount of pressure and … Holy Oprah. I *needed* to do it. Initially, I just reached up and started squeezing.

'What the hell?' he yelled, spinning around to face me.

'What?' I said, acting mystified and innocent. 'I was just clearing a blackhead for you.' How could he not appreciate my selfless and generous act?

'Well don't. That hurt.'

'No it didn't,' I said, turning him back around and forcing him into submission. 'Don't be a baby.'

I was repeating the trauma my own mother had put me through. I was a monster.

He let me squeeze a couple more that day. And the feeling I got, watching the blackhead come free, a tiny line of yellowish gunk snaking out behind it and leaving an empty, clean pore? Well, I'm fairly certain that's probably what heroin feels like. I became obsessed with squeezing his blackheads. I'd wait for him to fall asleep and shine a torch on his back, trying to get as many as I could before I woke him. I would do anything to chase that high. I started seeing them all over his body. My eyes had turned into a Terminator-like computer tracking system. Whenever I looked at him, I would scan his entire face and body and zero in on what blackheads could be attacked. He was no longer a human boyfriend to me. Just a walking, talking ecosystem of blackheads, waiting to be squeezed.

Funnily enough, that relationship didn't last, and I found myself, years later, thinking back to the sweet, sweet feeling of release I had for those few months I was getting high on his blackheads. Years later, when I found a way to satisfy my cravings online, I fell back into it with a little too much intensity. That first video I watched may or may not have led to a twelve-hour bender that I can't quite remember. But I do have a handle on it now. I can proudly say I only watch pimple-popping videos a few times a week. And definitely only for a few hours at a time.

I know for sure that at least one of the perfect Sarahs sitting sipping cocktails with me would be a secret pimple-popping watcher. I don't care how well vetted she was in 'what ladies should do' by the network's management. I can safely say, as a result of my own thoughts and assumptions, that at least eighty-five per cent of women get their jollies from squeezing other people's blackheads. It's one of the only legitimate reasons I would consider having a child.

Next disgusting truth bomb for the perfect, cocktail-sipping Sarahs in the TV show from my dreams: when I'm home alone, I take photos of any and all things I am curious about on my body but cannot see with the naked eye (usually due to my having the flexibility of an 85-year-old). If someone were to scroll through the photos on my phone, they'd inevitably come across about seven hundred photos of my vagina. These photos are sometimes about curiosity, sometimes about boredom, but mostly about an irrational fear I have that several debilitating things are constantly and simultaneously wrong with my lady garden.

('You just leave the photos on your phone? Isn't that just asking for trouble?' one of the Sarahs would ask. 'No!' I would say, swigging wine from the bottle now, 'because no woman can ever be blamed for the sexual assault perpetrated on her by a man! Including distributing images without her consent! Isn't this TV show we're on great! Now, what do you guys say we order some food?' All three perfect Sarahs: 'Food?')

I had cause to photograph my vag one day when I was walking through my local shops, looking to buy lunch with not a care in the world. Suddenly, I felt something abrasive against my labia. Like my undies were rubbing against it the wrong way or something. I tried to awkwardly readjust my underwear positioning by subtly shaking my leg out a few times as I walked, but to no avail. It really did feel like my undies were suddenly made of sandpaper. I made my way to the public bathroom to have a bit of a feel around down below. That's when I felt it – bulging just under the skin on the left labia majora (that's the outside flaps, fellas) was a marble-sized lump. Obviously I pulled my pants up immediately and hurried home to make a closer inspection. I lay down on my bed and felt around. There was only one of these lumps, but it was definitely there. I became convinced it was herpes, since I'd had a one-night stand a few months earlier, before I'd decided to take a break from random sex for a while (a girl needs to recharge every so often). We'd used protection, but I was sure the virus had jumped ship, latched onto one of my pubes until the coast was clear, then set up camp right in my vag. I took about fifty photos with my phone, trying to come at it from different angles so that I could get a clear picture that I could match to something on Google images. Eventually, I sent the best picture I had to my sisters, and broke the news to them that I was now a herpes carrier.

'That's not herpes,' Tayla immediately messaged back. 'It's just one random little thing. It's probably an ingrown hair.' (I knew it wasn't an ingrown hair. I'd had one of those before as well, and was convinced it also was herpes until I made Tony stick his head between my legs with a torch to have a closer look.)

Rhiannon said the same thing as Tayla. 'Rosie, if it was herpes, there'd be like, a cluster of scabs and stuff. That doesn't really look like anything. Just go to the doctor if you're worried.'

Going to the doctor with a vag problem is the worst possible thing on earth to do, except for maybe sitting through a conversation with a guy who constantly says 'NOT ALL MEN'. But I was concerned enough that I knew I had to suffer through it, so I made an appointment with the GP.

'Um, yeah,' I said, sitting in her office. 'I have, like, a vagina problem. There's a weird lump … on my vagina.' Ugh. Kill me please.

'Alright, well let's take a look at it then,' she said, gesturing towards the bed. Taking your pants off and getting on the bed is always such an awkward endeavour. It must be so much easier for guys, who can just pull their pants down and stand there. For women, you have to take your entire bottom half of clothing off, then you have to hoist yourself up onto the bed, lie back, and timidly spread your legs apart while you wait for the doctor to toddle on over. I always worry about toilet paper being stuck in my crack, which I've had a complex about since a boyfriend laughed himself out of bed during sex when he saw some three-ply wedged between my cheeks. (I found out later he'd told that story to a lot of people after we broke up, so I'd like to take this opportunity to say that he was basically a human jackhammer in bed.)

I reached down and pointed out my mystery lump to the doctor. It feels odd to say she 'fondled' it for a second, but it also feels like the most apt description: she fondled it for a second, told me she was done and went back to her desk. I slid off the bed as elegantly as I could (so not very), and put my pants back on.

She basically told me that I was being punished for having cut back on random sex with strangers. Well, that's how I chose to interpret it. It was something about a cyst that had formed because the glands that produce vag lubricant had become backed up with fluid. Backed up, I was certain, because I hadn't been using them enough. That's what I got for taking a sexual breather. She then informed me that the only way to get rid of the cyst was to take a week-long course of antibiotics, and if it hadn't disappeared by the end of that week, I'd need to go to hospital and have a needle inserted into my vag to drain out the excess fluid.

'I'm sorry, what?'

'You'll need to have the fluid drained, if it doesn't go down on its own,' she said.

'Yes, but, I'm sorry – I'm sure I heard you mention something about a *needle*? In my *vagina*?'

'That's how they drain the fluid.'

'Write me a prescription for the antibiotics immediately,' I said. No needle was going to be placed anywhere on or near my vagina.

I spent the week popping antibiotics while I obsessively took photos of my friendly neighbourhood cyst. My sisters got an update every day. Often I'd have the photoshoot lying down on the kitchen floor, because that room had the best light. I really wished there was some kind of online forum I could post the photos on, so I could get advice from women more supportive than my sisters, who had mostly taken to sending me back photos of rotten fish tacos, just to mess with my head.

When the cyst hadn't gone down after the first week, I demanded stronger drugs.

'I thought I told you not to mention the needle,' I said, when the doctor mentioned the needle.

'Listen, there has to be some other drugs we can try. They can't have been the strongest antibiotics on the market. What about the ones they use to, like, stop people's limbs falling off from infection in third world countries? Can I have one like that?'

'There is no drug like that.'

'Well if we can put a man on the moon, we can figure out a way to avoid putting a needle in my fucking vagina.'

She gave me a prescription for a stronger antibiotic, which worked. I'm sure I'm now resistant to all antibiotics and one day will die from a minor scratch, but I regret nothing.

At this point in our fun, cocktail banter scene during our fun, adorable network-show that definitely accurately portrays women, I'm sure the three perfect Sarahs would have left me alone at the table, the only woman who does actual disgusting and embarrassing stuff when she's home alone. I'd like to think, though, that at least one of those women went home to her perfect TV apartment in the perfect TV universe, stuck her hand down her pants, farted on it, then smelled it.

Or at least watched a pimple-popping video. I'd settle for that. Anything but reading *Vogue* while standing up in the kitchen eating crackers.

With your derrière ...

The nurse with my favourite Nikes had gone. She had been really pissed off when the enema poo exploded, because she wasn't wearing a mask and had copped a lot of it right in the face. I heard her bitching about it when I had been slowly wheeling my IV to the bathroom. I just figured she was lucky none of it got on her glorious shoes.

Something something something yeah.

It's Jack's Subway Tush.

Fuck. I couldn't decide what was more torturous: the constant dizziness that made me feel perpetually on the verge of puking, or not being able to nail down the words to that stupid fucking song.

I don't believe anything psychics say.
(I didn't, until something crazy happened.)
(And I know everyone says that their psychic story is crazy, but this was crazy.)

I didn't realise how stressful going to a psychic would be. In hindsight, that seems naïve on my part. I'm socially awkward at the best of times, so sitting face to face with someone I don't know while they hold my hand and stare straight into my eyes was bound to be unpleasant for me. But it wasn't so much the close proximity with an elderly woman dressed like a mystical hippie that stressed me out. It was my innate need to avoid any kind of awkward confrontation ever that made things really, really hard.

Let me put it this way: when you're sitting across from someone who's essentially trying to guess things about your life, and you have trouble saying no to people, you're going to end up confirming some crazy shit about yourself that is not even close to being true.

I just really didn't want Mystical Hippie Lady to feel bad. So within five minutes of sitting down, I had invented a dead grandmother called Melissa and got so caught up in a web of well-meaning lies that I felt like I needed to take a nap afterwards.

I sat down at her little table (covered in crystals, but none of the ball variety, which was disappointing, because naturally I expect every new experience in life to resemble a Disney movie), and waited in nervous silence while Mystical Hippie Lady lit a candle with what looked like a lighter that had been purchased at an off-brand 7-Eleven. I can see her now, walking into the store, head held high with the kind of dignity only someone with access to the other side can have. She'd stare intensely at the underpaid counter guy, tap her long fingernails on the counter and declare, 'Young man, I need something to light the candles I use to contact the souls of our ancestors.'

'We've got these fluoro ones,' he'd reply. 'Or there's one with Justin Bieber on it.'

Disappointed sigh. 'I'll take Bieber.'

She rummaged through her bag, pulled out her iPhone and set the timer. So mystical.

She picked up on something immediately. Lucky, since we only had twenty minutes.

'There's someone who's crossed over. She's here. Do you know a … It's definitely an "M" name. Or an "N" name. That's the sound I'm getting.'

'Melissa?' I offered, trying to end her desperate guessing.

'Yes! Melissa. It's definitely Melissa. So you know a Melissa who's passed?'

I didn't.

'Yes!' I whispered. 'I do!'

She looked very pleased with that.

'I feel like it's a female energy,' she said, successfully deducing that someone called Melissa may, in fact, have been female. 'Was it a … graaaan …'

She didn't seem to want to commit to finishing the word. I jumped in for her.

'Grandma?' I asked. 'Yep. I had a grandma called Melissa.'

I did not have a grandma called Melissa.

'What did she do for a living?' Mystical Hippie Lady asked. 'Was she … Was she …'

I threw her another bone. I just couldn't handle her awkward failure. It reminded me of when I used to cry as a kid watching *Mr Bean*. To me, that turkey on his head represented nothing but the abject failure of a hopeless man who would never amount to anything and would therefore die alone. I didn't understand why people found that funny. Arseholes.

'A writer?' I said.

My actual grandma did have a book published back in the day, so this was technically correct. Also, it was just easier for me at this point to start describing my real grandma, lest I get busted in my pity-induced lie.

'Yes!' she said. 'That's what I thought. Definitely a writer.'

Mystical Hippie Lady really felt like she was onto something now.

'She says that you wish you could be a writer too,' she said, winking at me.

'Um, well, I sort of write already,' I replied, definitely not returning her wink. I was just about to tell her that I actually write for a living, but I think by that stage she was amazing even herself with how well this was going. For the first time ever, she had lucked onto the right dead family member and the right name on the first go. She was feeling cocky now, so she cut me off before I could say anything about my writing career.

'No!' she said. 'Not just tinkering around with stuff. Not the way everybody with one of those blog things just says they're a writer. You actually want to be paid to write! You want it to be your career! What do you do for a living now?'

I was getting paid to write and it was my career. Oh god. *Mr Bean* was happening right in front of me, in real time. I couldn't take it. SAY SOMETHING, ROSIE.

'Um … I'm studying,' I said. 'Marketing?'

Nailed it.

'You need to change courses right now,' she said. 'You need to make a career out of writing just like your grandma Melissa. That's why she's here today – to tell you that if you make a change now, you could end up a paid writer within a few years. Just like she was.'

Well, I was in it now. I had to commit.

'That's so weird!' I said. 'My grandma Melissa always told me to be a writer!'

I may have been starting to believe grandma Melissa was real.

Satisfied that she now had enough information about me to wing it from that point, Mystical Hippie Lady went on to tell me about my past life (she could see me sitting on a stool, carving into stone – she decided this meant I was an important advisor to Ramesses II). Also that I wanted more affection out of my current relationship (I was single), and that I was going to move to Queensland because I love the sunshine (hate it, get burned walking to the bus stop, Queensland is my worst nightmare).

She finished up by reading some of my tarot cards, which all had to do with my grandma Melissa giving me certain pieces of advice, mostly about giving up marketing to become a writer.

Then, probably more confident about a reading than she ever had been in her life, Mystical Hippie Lady decided to try one more guess. But by this point I was so exhausted by the lies and the fake enthusiasm I couldn't keep it up anymore. It was time to let this hopeless, real-life Mr Bean spontaneously combust in front of me.

'Grandma Melissa is giving me some numbers,' she said, looking into the distance like she was seeing the numbers segment of Sesame Street right before her eyes. 'Do "7" and "10" mean something to you?'

'No.'

'How about "10" and "7"?'

'No.'

'107?'

'No.'

'710?'

'No.'

'There's no birthday on the 7th of October or the 10th of July?'

'No.'

There was an awkward silence. It was the first time in our iPhone-allotted twenty minutes that I had shot her down. I was just about to come to her rescue one final time, and make up something about my grandma Melissa being born on the 7th of October 1927, when Mystical Hippie Lady had her final brainwave.

'Oh. I understand. Melissa must be giving me those numbers because they're important. So just make sure you watch out for them. 7 and 10.'

And with that, Mystical Hippie Lady's Mystical iPhone beeped, and our twenty minutes was up. She looked incredibly pleased with herself. I wonder if she now uses our session as validation of her skills. At Christmas, when the family gets together and drunk cousin Peter is giving her shit for 'talking to ghosts wooooooooo' and everybody at the table laughs and shakes their heads at the life choices she's made, she can look back on our twenty minutes together and know that they can all get fucked, because she once made contact with that girl's grandma Melissa.

I, on the other hand, can look back and know that all it takes for me to turn into a pathological liar is twenty uncomfortable minutes alone with a well-meaning elderly woman.

There was one situation with a different psychic, though, in which I didn't have to fake anything. And it straight up gave me the heebie jeebies. Tony and I were attending a paranormal conference at an old 'haunted' jail. It went for two days, and covered everything from ghost hunting and alien abduction to time travel and past lives. Tony was obsessed with all of that stuff; he was a big believer. (Although the alien abduction seminar made even him uncomfortable – you can only listen to so many theories about aliens raping human women to use them as incubators to create a superhuman–alien hybrid race before you start to feel like maybe you're just indulging the delusions of someone who is very unwell. That, or these people really are at the forefront of an intergalactic space war and we had all better jump on board asap.)

Mostly, though, Tony was very enthusiastic about the whole weekend. He was a very spiritual person, the kind who believed that he was on another plane that most people just didn't understand. Which would drive me irrationally crazy. He once told me he'd seen a cut on someone's hand mend in front of his eyes just through the use of healing energy.

'You did not see that,' I said, immediately annoyed.

'Yes I did, Ro,' he replied. 'Energy is more powerful than most people realise. It can heal.'

'Tony. You did not see a cut close up right before your eyes. You just fucking didn't. If that actually happened, if someone was physically healed right in front of you just through the use of energy … how does that even work? The energy, I mean?'

'Someone who is trained to handle the toxic, broken energy in other people, takes their hands and rests them above the affected area. It takes years to learn how to take that toxic energy in through your hands and get rid of it safely for people.'

'So. So. So …' I was losing it. 'I can't … Oh my god, Tony. So you're saying that you witnessed a cut on someone physically heal right before your eyes, just because someone else waved their hands over it?'

'Yes, Ro! I saw the cut just close up! It was incredible.'

'You didn't fucking see that! And I tell you how I know you didn't – because if you actually saw someone physically heal right in front of you, just through the power of energy, then you basically witnessed the single most important medical advancement of our time. And I didn't see it on the fucking news, so I know you didn't see it.'

He was clearly getting frustrated with me at that point, and he was about to hit me with the 'it's just not on your level' argument, which always made me furious.

'Look, Ro, if you don't believe it then I don't know what to tell you. I think this stuff is only visible to the people who are open to it. Not everybody has the spiritual maturity to understand the potential in this world.'

'Get back to me when you see someone make a leg grow back.'

'Wanna watch *Real Housewives of Beverly Hills*?'

'Yes. Yes I do.'

Tony and I had an 'agree to disagree' arrangement when it came to the paranormal, with each of us feeling sorry for the other one and their misguided way of thinking. I couldn't think of anyone I would rather go to a paranormal conference with.

On the Saturday night, there was a special session with one of those people who talk to ghosts in front of everybody, but only ever through random symbols like: 'Does anybody in the room have a brown teddy bear at home? Your great aunt wants you to know that there's something important about your letterbox.' The only famous person I knew who did that kind of stuff was John Edwards, and nothing I'd seen of his had ever really convinced me beyond a reasonable doubt. I'm not saying I categorically deny the possibility of all that stuff, but I just want proof. If a ghost appears in front of me and can list the exact porn that I watch in secret, then yeah, I'll believe that ghosts exist.

The ghost whisperer we were lucky enough to witness was a woman, probably around fifty years old, and very ... normal looking. Just like the kind of woman you'd see in a supermarket, complaining to management about a fifty-cent price discrepancy on her favourite Weight Watchers brownies. Not what I was expecting at all.

Tony was beyond excited. He came from a huge Italian family and there were so many relatives he was hoping would 'come through'. It seemed like everyone in the room was hoping for certain relatives to come through. There was definitely an air of desperation and competition among the audience. There were only about thirty of us, but she made it very clear that she didn't control the messages – she just picked them up like a radio – so not everybody was going to get to chat to Grandpa.

She started 'picking things up' immediately, and none of it seemed impressive to me. The people who thought she was speaking about their relatives just seemed a little too eager to make the information fit. 'Someone over the left side of the room,' she'd say. 'An aunt who always wore a pink hat.' 'My sister's mother always wore a red cardigan?' the feeble response would come. 'Whoa,' Tony would say, amazed. I wasn't really feeling it.

Then she 'felt' something over our side of the room, in the row of seats that Tony and I were sitting in.

'It's someone's dad,' she said. 'The name starts with an "A".'

'Andrew?' someone hopefully called out.

'No, no. It's not Andrew,' she said, her face scrunched up like she was trying to solve a maths equation.

'Anthony!' Tony called out. 'Rosie's dad was called Anthony.'

'Yes!' she said. 'That's it! Anthony.'

I glared at Tony. I was in no mood to humour this obvious fraud of a woman in front of an audience.

'Oh,' she said. 'I'm so sorry. He killed himself.'

Wait, what …

'Um, yeah,' I said. 'He did.' I wasn't giving anything else away. I wanted to test this bitch.

'But … Wait, this is confusing,' she said, staring intently into nothing. 'He's … he's saying that he would have died anyway. Was he not well?'

I shrugged. I knew that he had cardiomyopathy from being a chronic alcoholic. When he was found, he had vomited all over himself and there was an empty bottle of pills next to him, but the autopsy revealed his heart wouldn't have lasted much longer anyway. I wasn't going to tell her that, though.

'It was his heart,' she said. 'From drinking. He drank too much.'

Well, holy shitballs. Tony was beaming from ear to ear. He couldn't deal.

'He's saying that your mum needs to be careful, that she's the same as him?'

My mum was also a chronic alcoholic.

'Oh! He's laughing now! He wants you to know that he saw the funny thing that happened in the car. Do you know what that's about?'

'Oh. My god,' said Tony. 'Something funny *did* happen in the car last night!'

Tony and I had borrowed my sister's car to drive to the conference. And the specifics of this are too humiliating to admit in detail, but let's just say we were taking selfies and nearly crashed into a tree. We couldn't stop laughing at what a shameful, stereotypically millennial way that would have been to die. We'd been laughing about it all day. But still, whatever. I didn't give her any details.

'He thinks you two are idiots,' she said, laughing.

Fair call. But still – Refusing. To. Engage.

'He's showing me a birthday cake. Is it your birthday soon?' she asked.

Goddamn it. Yes. My birthday was in two weeks.

'HER BIRTHDAY'S IN TWO WEEKS!' Tony squealed. He had officially lost it.

'Well he wants to say "Happy Birthday",' she said. 'And there's … Well, I don't know what this is … it's like … A toy, maybe? Like one of those trolls, I think. Those old troll dolls.'

Tony didn't know about this one, so he looked at me expectantly. Everyone in the room was looking at me, wanting so badly for it to mean something.

'Um, I dunno,' I said. 'That doesn't sound like anything to me.'

It did sound like something to me. She moved on to other people, and I sat there, in confused silence, thinking about my favourite present my dad had ever given me: a troll doll, but a special edition one with a crystal on its belly button. He gave it to me for my seventh birthday, and I still had it, sitting on a shelf at home in my bedroom.

When I told Tony later that night, he was hysterical with glee.

'WHAT? Why didn't you say anything! Rosie – this is it. This is proof. Your dad talked to you tonight. You have to believe now!'

But I was already finding ways to explain it all away. If Tony hadn't yelled out answers, she would have just changed what she was saying. 'Something funny in the car'? That could literally

247

be any car trip ever. If it hadn't been my birthday, it could have been someone else's – it's not that hard to think of someone you know who has a birthday coming up. And the troll doll … Well, I guess I looked like I was in my mid-twenties, which means that was probably a toy I would've played with as a kid, or at least would've known what it was.

See? IT WAS ALL A SHAM.

And I was happy to let it be a sham, I really was. If it had just been that one 'reading' that night, I would have easily written it off (much to Tony's frustration). But then something happened – and this is the crazy part. This is the part I can't explain. Please bear with me, because I know it sounds ridiculous.

When Tony and I got back to our apartment, after having been at the conference for two days, I walked into my room and stopped dead in my damn tracks. Right there, in the middle of my bedroom floor, standing upright, was the fucking troll doll.

I swear to Oprah.

The shelf it's normally placed on was on the other side of the room. It couldn't have fallen into that place on the floor. And besides, it was standing on its little troll feet – if it had fallen off the shelf, and somehow landed more than two metres away, it would not have landed on its goddamn little troll feet. I was still standing in the doorway of my bedroom, trying to logic my way around what I was looking at, when Tony looked over my shoulder.

He shrieked.

'Rosie! Fuck off! You did that!'

'Tony, I swear to Oprah I haven't moved from this spot. I saw it and I just stood here.'

The great thing about someone who believes is they just believe. I didn't need to convince him of anything.

'Oh my god, Ro, this is your dad,' he said earnestly. 'Your dad knew that you were doubting that he came through last night so he did this to convince you! This is your dad!'

I didn't know what to think. But I was freaked out enough to put the troll doll in the living room before I went to bed that night. And then I found myself on the Tony side of many conversations, trying to convince people that the 'troll doll incident' had actually happened.

'Rosie. That did not happen,' my friend Jamila said, rolling her eyes when I told the story.

'It did! I saw it! The troll doll was standing in the middle of my fucking room!'

'No it wasn't, Rosie. It wasn't.'

It is really annoying being on the non-sceptic side of that exchange. I *saw* it. I know what I saw. The only explanation that I can think of is that Tony wanted me to believe so badly that he somehow moved the troll doll. But we drove from the conference together, then we walked from the car to the apartment together, so I don't know when he could have done it. But that is the only logical explanation. He did really, really want me to believe.

He used to joke that if he died before me, I would be the first person he'd visit, just so he could finally win the argument. He promised to haunt me just to prove to me that spirits are real, thereby shoving it in my face.

After he died, I stayed up so many nights, begging him to do what he promised. 'Prove it to me, Tony,' I would cry into the darkness. 'Make some shit fly across the room! You fucking promised!'

I suppose the fact that I was even asking his ghost to throw my stuff around meant he had more of an influence on me than I realised. I believed enough to ask, at least.

Or maybe that's just hope. Whatever it is, he hasn't proven anything to me yet.

I'll always be waiting, though.

The nurse with my favourite Nikes had returned. She seemed to have recovered from being sprayed in the face with shit. Nurses really should be paid more than investment bankers. Note to self: when you get out of this hospital, write to someone about making sure nurses are paid more than investment bankers. Also, find out where she got her Nikes.

I'm okay.
(The biggest lie I've ever told.)

I'm okay. I'm okay. I'm okay. I'm okay.

That's what I kept telling myself, for weeks, after Tony's funeral.

As garbage overflowed in my kitchen.

I'm okay.

As vodka bottles rolled out from under my couch.

I'm okay.

As rotting food covered the plates that were piled up next to my bed.

I'm okay.

As every text, every phone call, every email filled me with dread.

I'm okay.

As my hair became matted from not showering.

I'm okay.

As I sat in the dark, in my bed, just staring. For hours and hours and hours.

I'm okay.

The day I walked into my apartment after attending Tony's funeral, I told myself that the next day would be better. From the next day, I would be okay. I had spent the two weeks after he died, in bed, letting grief freeze my life. But starting from tomorrow, I would get up, clean the apartment, get back to work, see the people I'd been avoiding. Starting from tomorrow, I'd get back to my life.

Then tomorrow came, and it still felt too hard. I didn't have the energy to get out of bed. I just wanted to sleep for a little while longer. Just a little while. But I'll definitely be okay tomorrow.

Then the next tomorrow came, and I was still so tired. My body had shut down. My brain was quiet. My heart was numb. One more day, Rosie, I'd tell myself, as I closed the blinds to shut out the sun. Indulge in this for one more day; then get up. Tomorrow you'll be okay.

I told myself that the next tomorrow and the next tomorrow and the next tomorrow and the next.

My agent would call me about work. 'I'm okay,' I'd say. 'I'll definitely get that done.' And in my head, I really thought I would. I'm still hiding today, but tomorrow I won't be, I thought. My publisher would call about the progress of this book. 'I'm okay!' I'd reply, no doubt in my mind that I would get started tomorrow. Mamamia, the website I freelanced for, would ask me about the recaps of *The Bachelor* I had to write. 'I'm okay,' I'd email back. 'So ready!' Certain that by then, the emptiness would be gone.

My friends called me, my sisters called me, my mum called me. 'I'm okay,' I'd say. 'I'm okay.' And I really thought I would be. I may be getting through today by hiding and sleeping and forcing myself to drink vodka even though it made me feel sick. But that's today. I just need to feel numb today.

I really thought every tomorrow would be the one where I would pull myself out of it.

I agreed to go to London, to attend and write about the world premiere of the new *Bridget Jones* movie – a kind of 'fish-out-of-water lol look at hilarious and awkward Rosie trying to fit in at a fancy premiere' kind of thing. 'Sure, I can do that,' I told my agent. It was still weeks away. By then I'd be okay. Definitely. London became my cut-off date. Get it together before London, Rosie. Be okay before London.

I sat in my apartment, trying desperately not to feel anything, while the world piled up around me. The few occasions I did venture out, I felt dizzy, and disoriented, like my brain could no longer function in the outside world. The sun irritated me, and just to walk felt exhausting. I needed to be inside. In my apartment. In my bedroom. In my bed.

As days stretched into weeks, I started to lose track of how long it had been. I would wake up, try to eat, add the plate to the floor of my bedroom. Then I'd sit in bed in a trance, for hours, cutting the bottoms of my feet. My sheets became stained with blood, but I didn't change them. I couldn't even be bothered changing my clothes. When there was no more left to cut, I kept picking, picking, picking at the skin, digging until my fingernails were brittle. I'd watch the same TV series I'd already seen over and over and over. *Seinfeld. The West Wing. 30 Rock. Frasier.* Anything I already knew every word of. Anything that would fill my brain without forcing it to think.

Late at night, when I couldn't sleep, I'd drink. But it wasn't for enjoyment, or to satisfy a craving. I would have to force myself to get drunk. It felt like a chore, but when the cutting was done, and the TV was done, I needed something to take over. I needed to be able to fall asleep without having to endure those painful silent minutes in the dark, waiting to drift off. There is nothing worse than the painful silence while you wait to fall asleep. It's an empty space just begging to be filled with the worst kind of thoughts. So I'd drink, and put the TV up as loud as it would go, filling the space up that way before any other thoughts could get in.

But I still kept convincing myself that I was okay. Just one more day like this, I'd say to myself. Just one more day in this bed. Tomorrow you'll be okay.

Then London was tomorrow.

I forced myself to shower, even though every bone in my body was begging me to lie back down. I washed my hair, I packed my suitcase, I posted an excited photo on Instagram. I was going to be okay. This was going to be okay.

I was flying business class, staying in a fancy hotel, going to a red carpet film premiere, and I was being paid for it. Plus, one of my best friends, Kate, lived in London, so I was sure this trip was going to snap me out of whatever ... funk had been going on with me. It *wasn't* my mental health – it was just a funk. I was grieving. I was a bit sad. But it was *not* my mental health.

My mental-health problems were in the past, and I was quite comfortable leaving them there. I had worked hard with a psychiatrist, for more than ten years, to deal with my PTSD and anxiety. I understood what triggers I needed to be careful about. I understood my severe childhood trauma meant my brain had developed differently to other people's. I understood that flashbacks, suicidal thoughts and dissociative behaviour were all symptoms I'd experienced, and talked and written about publicly. But I was happy to talk about them publicly in the *past tense only*. My mental-illness story was one of past recovery, not current struggle. 'Recovered' means it's over, I'm good now, I can talk about this because it's only in my past. That girl was a crazy lady. This girl is fine. I'm okay.

This definitely wasn't my mental illness. It definitely wasn't my PTSD or my anxiety. I'd just been in a funk, and now I was going to have fun in London and see my friend and everything would be okay.

For the first couple of days, it was. I completely flipped out over flying in business class, because I'd never done it before and couldn't believe how the other half had been living the entire time. Did you know there's a menu? And that you can order from it whenever you want? And somebody comes and gives you pyjamas and while you're changing into them they turn your seat INTO A BED? I was certain I was already starting to feel better (and I was now determined that my life reach a point of success that would ensure I'd never have to fly with the plebs in economy again).

I knew the premiere was meant to be fun, and it was, sort of – I looked sufficiently overwhelmed and awkward on the red carpet, which Kate photographed perfectly. But I just felt empty. Like a faker. I was mimicking having fun, but I didn't feel anything. Maybe it's just the premiere, I figured. You're not really a party person anyway. You'll start enjoying this when you hang out with Kate the next few days. She was going to show me around London, and I was glad that she was prepared to do every Tudor-themed tourist activity I had set my daggy heart on. I was outside, I had make-up on. My hair was washed. I was functioning, and I was doing it all on the other side of the world. I was going to be okay. Definitely going to be okay.

Then came the gastro.

After a sleep-in, I left my hotel the next day, planning on having a little stroll around on my own before meeting Kate for dinner and a show in the West End. I had requested traditional English pub food and *The Book of Mormon*. Perfect. Rosie was back.

I made it about halfway down the street when something really didn't feel right. I had the unmistakable sweetness in my mouth that suggested vomit was on its way. Also the unmistakable rumbling in my bowels that suggested poo was simultaneously on its way. I saw a McDonald's across the street. I looked back at my hotel, a few hundred metres away. I knew I could make it to the McDonald's, but with that came the risk of being stuck in the bathroom for an extended period of time (this did not feel like it was going to be a quick session). I could try for the hotel, where I'd have the safety of my room, but it was further away, so that came with the risk of not making it there at all.

I stood in the middle of that London street, something definitely about to burst out both ends of me, trying to decide on the best course of action.

I chose to make a break for the hotel. It was further away, but the idea of being stuck in that McDonald's bathroom, chained to a toilet by diarrhoea and/or vomit, was enough to make me risk it.

I hobbled down the street as quickly as a sick person can. I was breaking out in a cold sweat now. My whole body was clammy. This vomit was coming, and it was coming soon. I made it to the lobby of the hotel. My room was on level three, towards the back of the building. I stood, perfectly still, trying to will my body into holding everything in.

'Are you alright, Miss?' the doorman asked, clearly concerned.

I turned my head to face him. He looked into my eyes. I looked into his. We shared an odd moment of connection, as the whole world around us slowed down, and we both knew what was coming.

I spun around, faced the nearest wall and vomited. Violently. The doorman called for a cleaner, who came running out of nowhere with a bucket. I kept apologising. They kept asking if I needed a doctor. I didn't want to tell them that all I really needed at that moment was a toilet, because this was all about to happen again, except out the other end.

I insisted that I just needed my room, and a lovely staff member walked me there, which seemed thoughtful at the time, but in hindsight was probably just to make sure I didn't cover any more hotel surfaces in spew.

I barged into my room, ran to the toilet, and didn't leave its side for the next three days. Well, except to visit the doctor, who told me that I most likely had gastro, probably picked up at some point on my flight over from Melbourne. I couldn't believe my beloved business class had forsaken me.

Kate, brilliant friend that she is, went to the chemist and got me diarrhoea pills and water with electrolytes and called every day to see if I needed anything. I couldn't believe I was spending the bulk of my trip in London hugging the toilet and waiting for my friend to bring me anti-poop pills.

The day I was meant to fly home, I was no longer vomiting or pooping, but still felt very suspect. I had barely slept, and was sure I was dehydrated, but was hoping I'd just black out on the plane in that swanky business-class bed and feel much better by the time I got back to Melbourne.

I didn't sleep at all on the first leg of the trip, so at the stopover at Abu Dhabi airport I went looking for paracetamol – hopefully strong paracetamol that would guarantee I'd finally get some rest on the way to Melbourne. It was in a red box, surrounded by cheesy camel statues and genie lamps that were meant for white-lady tourists like me. 'EXTRA,' I thought, reading the box. That sounds intense. It's probably filled with codeine. 'Good. Perfect. That's what I need.' I was so out of it that I bought two genie lamps and a camel, then left them in the airport lounge.

I was thirsty, dizzy, tired. The crowds around me were starting to make me anxious. I wanted to get back to my bedroom. Something was wrong. My brain didn't feel right.

I took four of the fancy, intense 'EXTRA' paracetamol on the plane, but I didn't fall asleep. One of the flight attendants asked me at one point if I was okay. She said I looked distressed. I wasn't sure. I was tired, I told her. Just really tired.

By the time I landed back in Melbourne, I'd barely slept in three nights. I definitely hadn't slept at all in the last twenty-four hours. The taxi driver who took me home looked at me the same way the flight attendant had. He asked if I was okay, if I needed him to pull over. How bad could I actually look, I thought? I'm okay, I said. Just really tired.

I finally stepped back into my apartment. It smelled really bad. The garbage and plates and kitty litter I'd let pile up in the weeks before I left were still there. The blinds were still closed. Everything was dark. Tony's face flashed across my eyes. The plastic one. The face of the plastic doll in the chequered suit. I gasped, and leaned into the wall just inside the front door. I was dizzy. I felt faint, foggy. Like my brain needed glasses. I closed my eyes tight and kept shaking my head, trying to snap myself out of whatever was happening. The plastic face flashed in front of me again. Wait, was it in front of me? Or just in my mind's eye? My mind's eye, obviously. Definitely. Not actually in front of me. That would be crazy.

I went to my bedroom and crawled into bed. The sheets were still stained with blood from my cutting. The bed was still surrounded by plates. On one side of me, on the carpet, was dried vomit that I'd never bothered to clean up. I pulled the covers up over my head and tried to slow my breathing. The plastic face suddenly appeared in front of me again. Appeared, or flashed? Did I just picture it, or did I *see* it? What the hell was happening to me? It felt like I had never been to London. Now that I was back in my bed, it genuinely seemed like I had never left. My brain seemed to be rushing forward and back through time – was I going to London tomorrow, or had I just walked in the door? Was I dizzy because the walls were moving, or did it just seem like the walls were moving because I was dizzy? The plastic face. The chequered suit.

SLEEP, ROSIE. You have to sleep. Just sleep, and you'll be okay.

I drifted in and out, but I couldn't seem to sleep for more than an hour at a time. I couldn't tell how many days, if any, had passed. The walls were moving. I could swear that the bed was shaking. I couldn't stop seeing Tony's face, the cold, plastic face, in front of me. I tried watching TV; it didn't work. I tried drinking; it didn't work. I knew I couldn't be seeing what I was seeing. I was going to be okay. Things were going to be okay.

But what if they're not, Rosie? THE PLASTIC FACE. Your dad was diagnosed with schizophrenia in his early twenties, maybe it's come for you now. THE BED IS SHAKING. Maybe you've been crazy all along. THE CHEQUERED SUIT. Maybe this is just you – THE WALL IS MOVING – losing your mind.

Breathe, Rosie. Breathe. You're just tired. You'll be okay. It's going to be okay. You are okay.

I'm okay. I'm okay. I'm okay. I'm okay.

NOTHING IS OKAY, ROSIE. TONY IS DEAD. YOU ARE ALONE. HE WILL NEVER HOLD YOUR HAND AGAIN AND YOU WILL NEVER MAKE IT THROUGH LIFE WITHOUT HIM.

Everything stopped. My brain clicked into a false clarity.

Nothing is okay. Nothing will ever be okay. I know what I have to do.

I went and sat on the couch. I couldn't remember the last time I'd been out of my bedroom. I started to drink. Forcing down shots of vodka so fast it made me gag. When I couldn't do that anymore, I mixed it with just enough soda that it was drinkable. I kept going and going and going and going. Once I'd drunk all that I could bear, I knew what I needed to make me sleep. I just wanted to sleep, always. I wasn't okay. I wasn't going to be okay. My brain was broken. Tony was gone. I was losing my mind. I was crazy like my dad. I couldn't see a future in which I'd ever be able to leave this apartment.

Dying seemed logical. Dying seemed inevitable. Dying seemed … preferable.

This was how I would be okay. I was going to be okay.

I found the fancy, intense 'EXTRA' paracetamol I'd bought in Abu Dhabi. I knew death didn't come from regular headache pills, but these were strong.

Then I lay down and waited to sleep.

I'm not sure how long it was. Maybe fifteen minutes, maybe an hour – I'd lost all track of time. But all of a sudden, I was hit with a brutal, stabbing pain in my stomach. I gasped with pain. My skin started to burn and tingle, and my head seemed like it was filled with cement. I ran to the bathroom and threw up in the toilet, my stomach feeling like it was eating itself with every heave. I looked down into the bowl. It was bright green, like toxic waste had just come out of me. I stared at it, in a stupor, then it hit me.

Fuck.

What the fuck have I done? What fucking colour is that? FUCK.

Something about that bright green toilet bowl snapped me back to reality. I walked back over to the couch, sat down, and dialled my closest friend Jacob. He didn't answer. I dialled again. No answer. I called the next closest friend.

'Jamila,' I said. 'I'm not okay.' I finally said it to someone. 'I'm not okay.'

Things happened pretty quickly after that, or so I'm told. I can't remember anything until a few hours later in the hospital. I had, after all, consumed a lot of vodka, so I was wildly, ridiculously drunk.

Jamila's husband called an ambulance, and she met them at my apartment. Apparently, I spent the entire ride to the hospital giving a rather eloquent and heartfelt lecture about the failings of Australia's mental-healthcare system. So, you're welcome, overworked and underpaid ambos. I remember flashes of running to the bathroom. I remember feeling more sick than I'd ever felt in my life. Bright lights. Jamila stroking my hair. Almost collapsing before a nurse ran over and caught me. Something about finally reaching Jacob. Looking up and seeing I was in a bed. Needles, so many needles.

It turns out I had slept for more than an hour before I woke up and called Jamila, which meant it was too late to pump my stomach. So, I was just attached to a drip and told to wait. It was going to be at least sixteen hours. The nausea was like nothing I'd ever experienced before. Worse than being pregnant with Kate Middleton's vomiting disease. Imagine the most sick you've ever made yourself from drinking, but it lasts for three days. That's what my next three days were like. And because of the damn caffeine in the damn tablets, I couldn't just sleep through the worst of it. I just looked at Nikes and sang that damn Subway Tush song again and again and again and again.

But mentally, I was already feeling better. When the alcohol started to wear off and my brain could process regular human thoughts again, I could finally, for the first time in two months, look at what had been happening to me since Tony died. It was like I'd hit a reset button in my mind. I just felt so ... relieved. The first thing I was sure of is that I didn't want to die, and I was so glad the bright green toxic waste I'd hurled into my toilet snapped me out of myself enough to call someone. I had certainly wanted something to stop, but it wasn't my life. I think it was the pain, the grief, the fear, the exhaustion. Tony's death had triggered my PTSD in a way that it had not been triggered in a long time. Tony had been my family, my protector, my person. Tony was my person. And while I had been sure that the worst of my mental-health problems were behind me, I hadn't been tested by anything as traumatic as my childhood. Tony's death had tested me, and I had clearly not done so well.

But to stumble with your mental health is not a bad thing. I think I had become cocky about my mental health, and that needed to change. Mental illness will always be with me, and I can't pretend like things might not get that bad again. I needed to fall down to know that I could survive the fall. I almost didn't, but also, I did. Hopefully, if there's a next time, I'll be more prepared for it.

While I was in and out of lucidity, singing the wrong words to the Subway Tush song repeatedly, my friends wrapped around me in a circle of support. Mia paid for my younger sister Tayla to fly from Sydney to Melbourne to be with me. Dimity went and cleaned my apartment, which, let me tell you, can't have been easy. Jamila put her life on hold (husband and son included) to stay by my side. Jacob stopped working for a week to make sure I wouldn't be alone. Jenn flew my cat up to Sydney and had someone take care of him. Phill organised movers to take my stuff home, because Tayla agreed to let me move back into the apartment I had shared with Tony in Sydney.

There were so many brilliant people holding my hand.

The clearest memory I have after calling Jamila from my apartment is witnessing the enema poo blast, and Jacob's horrified face in the aftermath. He sat with me all day, leaving only when Jamila came to take over. Mia arrived from Sydney later that afternoon, and I had just been given an anti-nausea shot, so I had a bizarre conversation with her where I laughed and cracked jokes and acted like we were just hanging out in a coffee shop. Unfortunately, the cruelty of the anti-nausea shot is that it only lasts twenty minutes, so you get a brief glimpse of how good you could be feeling, before going back to needing to hurl repeatedly. I started leaning over the side of the bed towards the end of Mia's visit. She knew that was her cue to leave.

Before she left, though, she said to me, 'Rosie, next time this happens, you have to tell us what's going on. You need to reach out to someone on the way down. You need to tell us you're not okay.'

She had fear in her face. So did Jacob. Just as Jamila had the night before. And I'll never let go of the guilt I feel for making the people I love feel that fear. But I didn't know how to respond to Mia when she said that. How do you reach out on the way down when you don't even realising you're falling? Nobody wants to feel this bad. Nobody wants to get to the point I'd reached. If I thought I could stop it, or even that there was something to stop, I would have. Wouldn't I? I'd been suicidal before, during the worst periods of my PTSD, and I never imagined for a second that I'd end up there again. I, more than anyone, knew the signs. I knew when things were getting away from me. I knew when it felt like I was floating out into space with nothing to tether me down. When I said I was okay, I really didn't think I was lying. Because I really believed, or maybe just hoped, that I would be.

Until I wasn't.

'I know,' I said to Mia. 'I know. If it happens again, I'll say something.'

I didn't know how else to answer.

A psychologist was sent to see me, and I chatted to her for about ten minutes. I'd been in the public mental-health system before, and I knew it wasn't the place for me. She also knew they barely had space for the patients they already had, so she seemed relieved when I told her I was okay. 'I'm okay,' I said, and actually meant it for the first time in months. 'I'm really okay.' She said it was fine for me to go home. And I knew that it was.

I can't be sure how much time had passed by the time I left, but it got to the point where they were pretty desperate for me to free up the bed, and I was pretty desperate to get away from the curtain covered in shit. Jacob discharged me, I took one last look at that curtain, and we left.

'Jacob,' I said, in the Uber on the way to his house. 'I really want to buy a pair of Nikes tomorrow.'

Tayla and I stayed at Jacob's for a week, before we flew back to Sydney together. In treatment over the next month, I learned that I'd had a complete nervous breakdown, culminating in the night I tried to take my own life. After months of intense emotion bubbling under the surface, apparently the gastro, dehydration and lack of sleep had just tipped my brain over the edge. I was briefly hallucinating, but I wasn't schizophrenic. I wasn't turning into my dad. I wasn't the 'crazy lady' I had always feared. My body and mind just momentarily gave out, while under extreme pressure. My mental health had humbled me. I'm okay, but I also know now that I can't guarantee I always will be. But that's the best I can do. For now, I'm okay. Really.

Living back in Sydney, in my old apartment, with traces of Tony everywhere, I was finally able to process his loss, to allow myself to indulge in the memories I have of him, without fear of the pain being too unbearable.

I thought about the last time we ever spoke. I was sitting in the back of an Uber, having just gone to an audition for a major new Aussie TV show. Tony had been video-calling from Austin all week, practising my lines with me and convincing me I could do it. The night before, I was going to cancel because of nerves (and just, you know, my general chronic low self-esteem), but Tony wouldn't let me. Even from Austin, he was holding my hand. He was on the phone with me during the whole car ride to the audition, then, when I could no longer talk in the quiet waiting room, I started sending him sneaky photos of the other girls waiting to go in, lamenting about how beautiful they all were and how I was clearly the 'let's see if a chubby, funny girl could maybe work' random person on the audition list. He immediately drew farts coming out of all of their bums and sent the photos back to me. It wasn't a sophisticated method of support, but it definitely helped. It was the first professional acting audition I'd done since leaving drama school. I'd moved into writing and loved it and had just kind of accepted that the acting part had been left behind. I was petrified, but I got through it, only forgetting my lines out of sheer terror a couple of times.

I called Tony as soon as I was in the Uber coming home.

'Tonz, it was fucking awful!' I said. 'I was so bad! And all those other girls were so beautiful! And I forgot my lines! And I had to hold a tea-towel and I didn't know what the fuck to do with the tea-towel! Holy fucking Oprah, Tony. I was terrible.'

We laughed and laughed and laughed as I took him through every painful detail of how I screwed the whole thing up.

Then we talked about other stuff. Just random, normal stuff. His brother's wedding was coming up, and he was flying over so we could go to it together in Griffith. He had a bunch of job interviews that week in some bars and restaurants. He'd been swimming a lot in the pool at his apartment complex, and joked that he was turning into a fitness queen. I teased him about the drunk messages he'd sent me a few nights earlier. He teased me about my latest disastrous Tinder hook-up. Then, as the car pulled up to my apartment building, we started to say our goodbyes.

'Okay, love you boo,' he said. 'I'll call you soon about the deets for Joseph's wedding!'

'Okay boo, love you too. Miss you so much!'

'Miss you too!'

I was about to hang up.

'Wait, Ro!'

'What?' I asked, only half concentrating, trying to get out of the Uber.

'I really have a feeling about this show,' he said. I laughed. 'No seriously! I think you're going to get it, Ro. I just ... I know you're going to be on this show. You got this, Rosie. You got this.'

'Lol, I don't think so, but thanks boo,' I replied.

Then we hung up.

Not long after Tony died, I was offered a part on the show. I was also asked to be on the writing team, so basically my dream career from the time I was five years old.

Obviously, every day I went to work, I was petrified, because that's just my usual state of being. But I just kept telling myself what Tony had told me:

You got this, Rosie. You got this.

I'm not sure how I'm going to get through life without him holding my hand. But I know that I will. I may not do it perfectly. I may stumble again. (In fact, I will almost definitely stumble again.) But I will get through it. Tony's hand may not be there when I reach out for it anymore, but, in his infinite generosity and love, he left me with the exact words I need to get through each day without him.

You got this, Rosie. You got this.

When I think about Tony saying that, when I think how much he believed it, I feel okay.

And that's the truth.

(Oh and by the way... The day after I left hospital, I bought a pair of Nikes. I still don't know the words to that *Will & Grace* song. The outcome of the shit curtain remains unknown.)

Acknowledgements

Catherine Catherine Catherine. Catherine Milne, you wondrous goddess. I am so lucky to have you and your slightly panicked but always very supportive and loving emails. I could not have asked for a more kind and generous person to help through what ended up being a very different book to what I thought I would write. Thank you. Now let's start making some stuff up!

Kimberley Allsopp, you are the best publicist/drinking buddy a girl could ask for (especially when the drinks are on HarperCollins). Tony would be so glad that you are taking his place as my social safety blanket. You were his favourite.

Everyone else at HarperCollins, thank you so much for letting me work in the office so I could occasionally leave my bedroom and pretend to have a real job where I gossip around a water cooler. You guys feel like a family.

The Vic On The Park in Enmore, I wrote half of this book sitting at the corner table of the beer garden, so thank you. (And thank you to Piers for not minding when I got moved off that table and we ended up in a very awkward situation.) Also I love the pie with the mushy peas and gravy, so please always leave that on the menu.

Jennifer Naughton, I can't remember what my life was like before you were in it. From the day Tony dropped me off at your office I've felt so unconditionally supported. You believe in me and my career as much as he did. And as Tony would say: thank you so much for jumping on the Rosie Train! I don't know what I would do without you.

Jamila Rizvi and Jacob Stanley, you both grabbed my hands when Tony couldn't anymore. Thank you for being in my life and for laughing with me and cleaning my burned bum and buying me pyjamas.

Mama, Rhiannon, Tayla, Isabella, Allira and Mohammed (and now Aya!). The little family unit we've created is hilarious and perfect. Let's keep tagging each other in memes that Mum doesn't understand.

And to my second, brilliant family:

Pat and Mary, Franky, Sarina and Bruno, Joseph and Melissa, and Francesca, Joseph, Marissa and Patty. And the nonnas! And Assunta! And the cousins and the aunts and the uncles! All of you.

It has been the greatest privilege of my life to be accepted into your fold. You have made me feel like I will always have a home to go to in Griffith, and I'll never be able to adequately convey how grateful I am for that.

Although this has been a story about my grief at losing the brilliant man you all played a part in creating, I also, as best as I could, tried to make it a story about the man. And what a man he was. Antonio Paul Sergi was incomparable, magical, incredible. And that's because of all of you.

Always look up.

Resources

If you're going through tough times and feel like you need some help, there are places and people who can support you. It's always a good idea to talk to someone you trust – you don't have to go through this alone. Contact a helpline, your GP, a counsellor, psychologist or psychiatrist, a hospital emergency department, minister, teacher or anyone you trust to keep you safe. Below are some places to go to for information and support:

- Lifeline: 13 11 14 (available 24/7) or Online Crisis Support Chat (available nightly at www.lifeline.org.au)
- SANE Australia (www.sane.org) 1800 18 7263
- headspace (www.eheadspace.org.au) 1800 650 890
- Kids Helpline (kidshelpline.com.au) 1800 551 800
- Reach Out (www.au.reachout.com) online youth mental health and wellbeing service
- Beyondblue Support Service (www.beyondblue.org.au) 1300 22 4636
- MindSpot Clinic (mindspot.org.au) 1800 61 44 34
- Qlife (qlife.org.au),a counselling and referral service for people who are LGBTI: 1800 184 527
- Suicide Call Back Service: 1300 65 94 67
- If your life is in danger – call emergency services 000